Great American History Games

By Lorraine Hopping Egan
and Louise Spigarelli

SCHOLASTIC
PROFESSIONAL BOOKS

New York • Toronto • London • Auckland • Sydney
Mexico City • New Delhi • Hong Kong

Dedication

Many thanks to the hardworking (and hard-playing!)
middle school students at St. Mel's who helped to
debug and greatly improve these games.

Acknowledgment

Special thanks to Bill Singer and his fifth graders at
Miraloma Elementary School for testing several of the games in this book.

Fact checking by Jeanne Rosenblatt

Cover design by Norma Ortiz
Interior design by Sydney Wright
Interior illustrations by Mona Mark and Norma Ortiz (page 9)

ISBN 0-439-11104-8

Contents

Introduction 4

CHAPTER 1
PEOPLE AND PLACES

Name That Face!
investigating historic figures 5/poster

Portrait Story
linking creative writing and biography 9

Democracy Speaks: Quotation Bingo
exploring quotations about democratic ideals 10

State Capital Map Search Game
understanding geographic history 17

Place-Name Scavenger Hunt
discovering patterns in movement and exploration . .22

Passport to America Game
understanding immigration across the centuries . . .25

CHAPTER 2
COLONIAL AMERICA

**Courageous Colony: A Colonial
Survival Board Game**
simulating the Jamestown experience 35/poster

**Hear Ye! Hear Ye! Revolutionary War
News Game**
gathering evidence to understand historic events . . .39

**Spy Versus Spy: Revolutionary War
Research Game**
conducting biographical research 48

Law of the Land Scavenger Hunt
using a primary source: the U.S. Constitution 53

CHAPTER 3
EAST TO WEST, NORTH VERSUS SOUTH

**West Quest 1, 2, and 3:
Time-Line Puzzles**
building a chronology of westward movement 57

North or South? Civil War Fact Game
classifying historic events and figures 63

**Battle of the Brains: Civil War
Question-and-Answer Game**
exploring historic events and figures 65

**Spy Versus Spy: Civil War
Research Game**
conducting biographical research 71

CHAPTER 4
THE PROGRESSIVE ERA

**Muckraker: A Progressive Era
Board Game**
investigating historic events and figures 73

Poster Side 1: **Faces in American History**
and **Courageous Colony Board Game**

Poster Side 2: **History Mystery Puzzles**
teacher page and answer key

History Mystery Puzzles: Strategies & Tips
student reproducible

History Mystery Puzzles:
July 4, 1776 (Declaration of Independence)
December 14, 1777 (Valley Forge)
1833 (Slavery)
January 24, 1848 (Gold Rush)
April 8, 1861 (Fort Sumter)
1896 (The Gold Standard)

Note: For learning goals keyed to national social studies standards, see the "Objectives" listed for each game or activity.

Introduction

Make it stick. That's my greatest challenge as a social studies teacher. Repetition and review may help students remember what they've learned. But there's also a fun way for kids to learn history: through games, puzzles, and other creative projects.

Over the course of a year, I teamed up with veteran education writer and game inventor, Lorraine Hopping Egan, to create a set of *Great American History Games* designed to motivate my students and to enhance my American history curriculum. My students have tested them all, and they really work.

These are the games my students ask . . . make that beg . . . to play. In a Jamestown simulation game (page 35), students overcome hardships as they work their way up from indentured servitude to gentry status. As town criers, they piece together news stories about famous events in the American Revolution (page 39). As undercover agents, they research the secret identities of Confederate and Union spies (page 71). My students often ask to take home the most popular games such as Passport to America (page 25), North or South? (page 63), and the Muckraker board game (page 73). They find the History Mystery Puzzles (poster) "hard in a good way," and yet they come back for more.

This is the material my students remember. I often hear them refer to a game when trying to remember facts or ideas, such as the gist of the First Amendment or events that led to the Mexican War.

This is the book that makes it easy for you. We've researched and developed pages of reproducible question and fact cards, research forms, game boards, puzzles, news stories, famous quotations, and even "passports" of 24 immigrants. All you have to do is photocopy, cut out, and laminate.

We've included rule variations and questions on two levels of difficulty for use in fifth through eighth grades, the prime years in which American history is taught.

And whether you are a teacher with 30-plus students or a home schooler with one or two children, you'll find game variations to accommodate the size of your student group.

For those who have access to the Internet, we've included a number of Web links for teachers and children.*

Feeling creative yourself? Please take our recipes for success and add your own special touches. We'd love to hear how you spice, dice, and remold them. Contact us c/o Scholastic Professional Books, 555 Broadway, New York, NY 10012, or at hopping9@mail.idt.net.

—Louise Spigarelli

*Web addresses often change or disappear. However, if an address doesn't take you where you want to go: retype it and try accessing it again; type in only the domain (e.g., www.scholastic.com) and navigate from the home page to the desired pages by clicking on topics; or use a search engine to search for key words in the address or Web site topic.

Name That Face!

✦ A Biographical Research and Guessing Game ✦

Players use prior knowledge, clues, and
research skills to identify pictures of important figures
featured on the Faces in American History poster.
This game provides a perfect motivator to get kids into class
by investigating the clues you post each day.

Materials

Players: any number

- ♔ Faces in American History (poster included with this book)
- ♔ Name That Face! Clue Cards (page 8)
- ♔ American history references
- ♔ (Optional) Internet access, Portrait Story reproducible (page 9, pregame activity)

Objectives

Historical Perspective (Comprehending the Past):
Investigate and identify primary-source photographs of individuals in history. Describe how the individuals influenced events in American history.

Language Arts: Observe, describe, and interpret photographs to write a creative short story, biography, or letter (Portrait Story pregame activity).

Preparation

✸ Laminate and post the Faces in American History poster.

✸ Copy and cut out the clue cards (page 8) and each

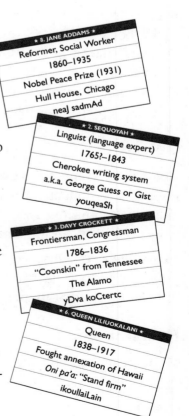

★ 1. ABIGAIL ADAMS ★
First Lady (born "Smith")
1744–1818
Colonial independence
Women's rights
ilabgAi mAdsa

★ 7. CHIEF JOSEPH ★
Nez Percé Leader
1840–1904
1,000-mile escape to Canada
"I will fight no more forever."
ifeCh eshoJp

★ 4. SOJOURNER TRUTH ★
Abolitionist, Preacher
1797–1883
Freed slave
". . . and ain't I a woman?"
erronuSjo hurtT

★ 5. JOHN BROWN ★
Abolitionist
1800–1859
Harper's Ferry rebellion
Hanged and martyred
nJho wroBn

★ 8. JANE ADDAMS ★
Reformer, Social Worker
1860–1935
Nobel Peace Prize (1931)
Hull House, Chicago
neaJ sadmAd

★ 2. SEQUOYAH ★
Linguist (language expert)
1765?–1843
Cherokee writing system
a.k.a. George Guess or Gist
youqeaSh

★ 3. DAVY CROCKETT ★
Frontiersman, Congressman
1786–1836
"Coonskin" from Tennessee
The Alamo
yDva koCtertc

★ 6. QUEEN LILIUOKALANI ★
Queen
1838–1917
Fought annexation of Hawaii
Oni pa'a: "Stand firm"
ikoullaiLain

clue. Cover each name on the poster with any of the five clues for that person.

3 (Optional) Make one copy per student of the Portrait Story reproducible. Have students do this observation and writing activity before playing Name That Face! (i.e., before they know the identities of the individuals). Instead of writing a short story, students can create a dialogue with the person or write a short fictional biography.

How to Play the Game

1 Each day, post a new clue for every person on the poster and challenge students to identify all eight famous people in American history by the end of five days. (Students can use almanacs, biographies, textbooks, the Internet, or other pertinent reference sources.)

2 Once a student has identified a featured person on the poster, he or she should secretly check the answer with you and, if correct, allow others in the class to discover the answer on their own.

3 At the end of the fifth day, remove the last clues from the poster to reveal the names. Ask: How many names do students recognize? How many did they learn while playing the game? What other facts did they uncover about the individuals?

Variations

More Portraits: Locate and post images and clues for other famous Americans. (See "Web Links." Beware of copyright restrictions when printing images from Web sites.)

Current Events: Newsmagazines often have large portraits of well-known people on their covers or in feature stories. Use these portraits to play a current events version of Name That Face! Add news headlines to biographical clues.

Puzzle Portraits: Using portraits that you have cut out of magazines, printed from the Internet or software programs, or copied from other sources, laminate and cut each portrait into five puzzle pieces. Post one piece of each puzzle per day. Challenge students to use visual clues to identify the people before their entire portraits are assembled.

Extensions

Name That Place: Locate pictures of famous landmarks in travel and cultural magazines such as *National Geographic* and post them on a bul-

letin board. Cover each picture entirely with three to five clue cards. Remove one card each day. Who can guess the landmark's name and location before the picture is revealed?

Internet Search: Challenge students to use the Internet or other references to find at least one contemporary of each person on the poster. They could alternately locate someone in history who shares their birthday. Another option is to have students use the information they uncover to write three to five clues about a famous person and challenge their classmates to guess who it is.

A&E Biographies: www.AandE.com or biography.com
Online biographies based on the popular cable program.

Civil War Biographies: civilwarhome.com/biograph.htm
Background information and historic images.

Early America: www.earlyamerica.com/portraits/index.html
Images and short bios of presidents, patriots, military leaders, and other men (no women) from the 17th and 18th centuries.

History Place: www.historyplace.com
Images and information covering the Civil War, Revolutionary War, explorers, colonial America, and more.

National Press Club's Library: www.press.org/what/library/index.html
Thorough and useful bibliography of Internet references, including biographical databases. Created for journalists, but accessible to all.

Library of Congress: American Memory: memory.loc.gov
Images, lesson plans, primary-source documents, and more. Also check out *Eyes of the Nation: A Visual History of the United States* by Curators of the Library of Congress (Knopf, 1997).

PBS's *The West*: www.pbs.org/weta/thewest/
Images of both famous and unknown people. Click on "Archives."

Presidents and First Ladies (images):
www2.whitehouse.gov/WH/Welcome.html
Click on "White House History and Tours." Also check out "The White House for Kids."

U.S. Civil War Center: www.cwc.lsu.edu/cwc/links/photo.htm#Photodex
Dozens of links to sources of Civil War photos.

BOOK LINKS

Civil War Military Leaders in Photographs: 24 Cards by Matthew Brady (Dover, 1998)
Inexpensive set of cards by the premier photographer of the Civil War. Also look in your library for other photograph books by Brady.

Hidden Witness: African-American Images from the Dawn of Photography to the Civil War by Jackie Napolean Wilson (St. Martin, 1999)

Touched by Fire: A National Historical Society Photographic Portrait of the Civil War by William C. Davis (Black Dog & Leventhal, 1997)
We found this normally expensive book in the bargain section. Also check your library.

Witness to an Era: The Life and Photographs of Alexander Gardner by Mark Katz (Rutledge Hill, 1999)

Name That Face! Clue Cards

★ 1. ABIGAIL ADAMS ★	★ 2. SEQUOYAH ★
First Lady (born "Smith")	Linguist (language expert)
1744–1818	1765?–1843
Colonial independence	Cherokee writing system
Women's rights	a.k.a. George Guess or Gist
ilabgAi mAdsa	youqeaSh
★ 3. DAVY CROCKETT ★	★ 4. SOJOURNER TRUTH ★
Frontiersman, Congressman	Abolitionist, Preacher
1786–1836	1797–1883
"Coonskin" from Tennessee	Freed slave
The Alamo	". . . and ain't I a woman?"
yDva koCtertc	erronuSjo hurtT
★ 5. JOHN BROWN ★	★ 6. QUEEN LILIUOKALANI ★
Abolitionist	Queen
1800–1859	1838–1917
Harper's Ferry rebellion	Fought annexation of Hawaii
Hanged and martyred	*Oni pa'a:* "Stand firm"
nJho wroBn	ikoullaiLain
★ 7. CHIEF JOSEPH ★	★ 8. JANE ADDAMS ★
Nez Percé Leader	Reformer, Social Worker
1840–1904	1860–1935
1,000-mile escape to Canada	Nobel Peace Prize (1931)
"I will fight no more forever."	Hull House, Chicago
ifeCh eshoJp	neaJ sadmAd

Portrait Story

An Observation and Writing Activity

Directions: Choose any one of the eight portraits on the Faces in American History poster. Study the portrait closely. Then use your observations and your imagination to answer the questions below. On the back, write a short story about the person.

OBSERVATION QUESTIONS

1 Describe the clothing the person is wearing. Does he or she have any jewelry, decorations, or accessories? If so, describe them.

_____

_____

2 Look at the person's facial expression and try to imitate (copy) it. What emotion was he or she feeling when the portrait was made?

_____

_____

3 What else do you notice about the portrait? Do you see anything unusual, odd, interesting, or mysterious?

_____

_____

IMAGINATION QUESTIONS

4 Describe the person's character. Do you think this person was generally happy or sad? kind or mean? friendly or not friendly? lucky or unlucky?

_____

_____

5 What do you think the person might have done for a living?

_____

_____

6 What type of home might he or she have lived in? Where was it located?

_____

_____

Democracy Speaks:

Quotation Bingo

❦ A Historic Quotation Game ❦

Players match quotations with speakers on a bingo card.

Materials

Players: 2 or more players, plus a game monitor

♔ Quotation Bingo Wise Words Quotations (pages 13 and 14)
♔ Quotation Bingo Game Boards (pages 15 and 16)
♔ small place markers (6 per player)

Objectives

Civic Perspective (Ideals of American Democracy): Acquire information through primary sources about core democratic values such as liberty, equality, patriotism, justice, and civic unity.

Language Arts: Interpret, classify, and explain quotations.

Fine Arts: Design and illustrate a poster (extension).

Preparation

1. The quotations express themes of unity, freedom, justice, equality, and duty at different points in American history. Prior to playing the game, write each theme topic on the board, leaving room underneath for students to post comments. Discuss the meanings of the theme words.

2. Copy the quotation list (pages 13 and 14) and cut apart the quotations. (Keep the speakers' names attached.) Divide the quotations evenly among groups of three or four students.

3. Ask each group to read their quotations aloud and post them under the theme categories. Some quotations fall into more than one category; the group should decide where to put them.

4. Read and discuss with the class the quotations in each category:

UNITY: *E pluribus unum* is our nation's motto. What other quotations are about a unified versus a divided country? (*Carter, Franklin, Holmes, Jackson, Lazarus, Lincoln, Webster, Willkie, Wilson*) At what points in history did this issue become especially important? (*Revolutionary War, Civil War, during times of heavy immigration*)

How has the image of America changed? Is America a melting pot, as many 19th-century leaders

like Teddy Roosevelt believed, or is it, according to many current leaders, more like a multi-faceted mosaic (Jimmy Carter) or rainbow (Jesse Jackson)? Besides immigrants, what other groups can be unified? (*Anthony—unity of women, Grimké—unity of men and women, Hutchinson—unity by religious beliefs, Chief Joseph and Chief Seattle—unity of one's people*)

FREEDOM: Patrick Henry said, "Give me liberty or give me death!" Compare his quotation to that of Harriet Tubman. Were they talking about the same thing? Why or why not? What does Frederick Douglass mean in his third quotation? How does enslaving one person enslave everybody?

JUSTICE: Justice is about treating people fairly. Which quotations are about injustices? Against whom? (*Addams and Mother Jones—children; Black Hawk, Chief Joseph, Chief Seattle, and Sitting Bull—Native Americans; Douglass, King, Lincoln, and Truth—African Americans; Keller—class or social standing; Sherman—victims of war; Tarbell—the poor and unemployed; Thoreau—citizens of an unjust government*)

DUTY: Duty is a personal responsibility, such as a duty to serve a country in time of war. Which quotations are about duty to country? (*John Adams, Hale, Henry, Kennedy, Lincoln, Paine, Sherman, Washington, and Wilson*) Which ones are about duty to things other than country? (*Jane Addams and Tarbell—ethics or morals, Hutchinson—religious beliefs*)

EQUALITY: Jefferson wrote in the Declaration of Independence that "all men are created equal." Compare this quotation to similar ones by Stanton and Stowe. What other quotations mention "equal" or "equality"? Between whom? (*A. Adams, Grimké, and Stanton—men and women; Chief Joseph and Sitting Bull—Native Americans and white people; S. Jones—rich and poor; Douglass and King—African Americans and Caucasians; Keller and Tarbell—classes*)

✴ Copy and cut out one bingo card (pages 15 and 16) per player.

✴ Gather the quotations and place them in a container for a random drawing. Alternatively, provide a full-page copy of the quotations to the game monitor.

✴ If you are playing with permanent boards, distribute place markers such as washers, dried pasta, or pieces from old games (Risk® cubes or Monopoly® houses, for example).

How to Play the Game

✴ The game monitor chooses a quotation from the list and checks it off or draws a quotation at random. The monitor reads it aloud, including the date (the monitor should not read the speaker's name).

✴ If players have the speaker on their card, they cover it with a place marker. If the speaker is a president, players can cover the center space ("Any U.S. President") and, if their card has it, the president's name. Most students will figure out that the date of the quotation has to fall within the life span of the speaker (provided on the bingo cards). To make the game easier, the game monitor can also give the context of the quotation by reading the speaker's title and the time period (e.g.,"During the Revolutionary War, a patriot said . . .").

❸ The game monitor reads quotations until a player has three speakers in a row—up and down, side to side, or diagonally. The game monitor checks the card for accuracy and either proclaims a winner or, if a mistake is found, continues reading quotations.

Variations

Longer Version: The winner must cover all nine spaces of a bingo card. Another variation is to cover all four corners and the center.

Add Quotations: Have students research the people on the bingo cards to find quotations to add to the list.

Fact-Based Version: Instead of quotations, have students generate clues to identify the people on the bingo cards. For example, "She was arrested in 1872 for casting a vote." (Susan B. Anthony)

Extension

Theme Poster: Have students create a poster of quotations and illustrations based on one of the themes.

American Slave Narratives:
xroads.virginia.edu/~hyper/wpa/wpahome.html
Newspaper articles, interviews with ex-slaves, and sound files.

Bartleby Library: www.bartleby.com
Online books, alphabetical by author, and quotations. Click on "Simpson's Contemporary Quotations" or "Bartlette's Familiar Quotations."

Eye Witness: www.ibiscom.com/index.html
Online samples from a software publisher of primary documents about historical events.

Library of Congress: American Memory: lcweb2.loc.gov/ammem/
Numerous primary documents, lesson plans, and links. Also includes the complete collection of Abraham Lincoln papers at memory.loc.gov/ammem/alhtml/malhome.html

Martin Luther King's Washington Speeches:
www.webcorp.com/civilrights/mlkfr.htm

U.S. Historical Documents: w3.one.net/~mweiler/ushda/ushda.htm
Searchable speeches, addresses, and famous documents.

U.S. Historical Documents on Slavery: www.bungi.com/cfip/slavery.htm
Links to primary documents, including court decisions.

BOOK LINKS

American Indian Quotations, ed. by Howard Langer (Greenwood Publishing, 1996). About 800 quotations spanning four centuries, from the 1600s the present.

American Quotations, ed. by Gorton Carruth and Eugene Ehrlich (Random House, 1994).

Eyewitness to America, ed. by David Colbert (Random House, 1997). Primary documents, from Columbus to Clinton.

Scholastic Treasury of Quotations for Children, by Adrienne Betz (Scholastic, 1998). About 1,200 quotes in 70 categories.

Quotation Bingo Wise Word Quotations

| ✓ | SPEAKER | QUOTATION |

✓	SPEAKER	QUOTATION	✓	SPEAKER	QUOTATION
☐	**Abigail Adams** First Lady	In the new code of laws . . . remember the ladies. (Letter to J. Adams, 1776)	☐	**Angelina Grimké** Women's Rights Leader	I recognize no rights but human rights. I know nothing of men's rights and women's rights. (Letter, 1837)
☐	**John Adams** U.S. President	The die was now cast . . . Swim or sink, live or die, survive or perish with my country . . . (Conversation, 1774)	☐	***Nathan Hale** Patriot	I only regret that I have but one life to lose for my country. (Just before hanging as a patriot spy, 1776)
☐	***Adams, Jefferson** <u>U.S. Presidents</u> **Franklin** Statesman	*E pluribus unum.* (Out of many, one. Motto for the seal of the United States.)	☐	***Patrick Henry** Patriot and Statesman	Give me liberty or give me death! (Speech to Virginia convention, 1776)
☐	**Jane Addams** Social Reformer	Action is indeed the sole medium of expression for ethics. (Writings, 1902)	☐	**Oliver Wendell Holmes, Sr.** Writer	One flag, one land, one heart . . . One Nation, evermore! (Civil War speech, 1862; son was a Supreme Court justice)
☐	**Susan B. Anthony** Women's Rights Leader	Join the union, girls, and together say "Equal Pay for Equal Work." (*The Revolution*, 1869)	☐	**Anne Hutchinson** Religious Leader	Take heed how you proceed against me, for . . . God will ruin you and your posterity, and this whole state. (Before exile from Massachusetts Bay colony, 1637)
☐	**Susan B. Anthony** Women's Rights Leader	Men their rights and nothing more; women their rights and nothing less. (*The Revolution*, 1868)	☐	**Jesse Jackson** Civil Rights Leader	Our flag is red, white, and blue, but our nation is a rainbow—red, yellow, brown, black, and white. (Speech, July 1984)
☐	**Black Hawk** Sac Leader	An Indian who is as bad as the white men could not live in our nation. He would be put to death, and eat up by the wolves. (Speech, 1835)	☐	***Thomas Jefferson** U.S. President	We hold these truths to be self-evident, that all men are created equal . . . (Declaration of Independence, July 2, 1776)
☐	**Jimmy Carter** U.S. President	We become not a melting pot but a beautiful mosaic. Different people, different beliefs, different yearnings, different hopes, different dreams. (Speech, 1976)	☐	**Mother Jones** Labor Reformer	Philadelphia's mansions were built on the broken bones, the quivering hearts, and drooping heads of these children. (Washington protest march, 1903)
☐	**Frederick Douglass** Abolitionist	You have seen how a man was made a slave; you shall see how a slave was made a man. (Writings, 1845)	☐	**Samuel M. Jones** Labor Reformer	Shall we have the golden rule of all the people or the rule of cash by a few people? (1897)
☐	**Frederick Douglass** Abolitionist	The destiny of the colored American . . . is the destiny of America. (Civil War Speech, 1862)	☐	***Chief Joseph** Nez Percé Leader	From where the sun now stands, I will fight no more forever. (Surrender, 1877)
☐	**Frederick Douglass** Abolitionist	No man can put a chain about the ankle of his fellow man without at last finding the other end fastened about his own neck. (Speech, 1883)	☐	***Chief Joseph** Nez Percé Leader	We only ask an even chance to live as other men live. We ask to be recognized as men. We ask that the same law shall work alike on all men. (Article, 1879)
☐	***Benjamin Franklin** Statesman	We must all hang together, or assuredly we shall all hang separately. (Letter, July 4, 1776)	☐	**Helen Keller** Political Writer	There is no king who has not had a slave among his ancestors, and no slave who has not had a king among his. (*The Story of My Life*, 1902)

* Starred items might be most familiar to students

Quotation Bingo Wise Word Quotations

✓	SPEAKER	QUOTATION	✓	SPEAKER	QUOTATION
☐	***John F. Kennedy** U.S. President	My fellow Americans; ask not what your country can do for you; ask what you can do for your country (Inaugural Address, January 20, 1961)	☐	**Harriet Beecher Stowe** Writer	All men are free and equal in the grave, if it comes to that. (*Uncle Tom's Cabin*, 1852)
☐	***Martin Luther King, Jr.** Civil Rights Leader	I have a dream that one day this nation will rise up and live out the true meaning of its creed: "We hold these truths to be self-evident; that all men are created equal." (Speech, 1963)	☐	**Ida Tarbell** Writer and Social Reformer	Many men . . . tell us the unemployed have always been with us, and always must be. It is the oldest reason in the world for tolerating injustice and misery. (Writings, 1914)
☐	**Martin Luther King, Jr.** Civil Rights Leader	Injustice anywhere is a threat to justice everywhere. (Letter from jail cell, 1963)	☐	**Sojourner Truth** Abolitionist	If my cup won't hold but a pint and yourn holds a quart, wouldn't ye be mean not to let me have my little half-measure? (1851)
☐	***Emma Lazarus** Writer and Poet	Give me your tired, your poor,/Your huddled masses yearning to breathe free . . . ("The New Colossus," 1883, quoted on the Statue of Liberty)	☐	**Sojourner Truth** Abolitionist	Look at me! Look at my arm. I have plowed, and I have planted . . . and ain't I a woman? (Women's Rights speech, 1851)
☐	**Abraham Lincoln** U.S. President	The ballot is stronger than the bullet. (Speech on democracy, 1856)	☐	**Henry David Thoreau** Writer	Under a government which imprisons any unjustly, the true place for a just man is also a prison. (*Civil Disobedience*, 1849)
☐	***Abraham Lincoln** U.S. President	A house divided against itself cannot stand. I believe this government cannot endure permanently half slave and half free. (Speech to Republican Convention, 1858)	☐	***Harriet Tubman** Abolitionist	There was one of two things I had a right to: liberty or death. If I could not have one, I would have the other, for no man should take me alive. (*Harriet, Moses of Her People*, 1869)
☐	**Abraham Lincoln** U.S. President	If slavery is not wrong, nothing is wrong. (Letter, 1864)	☐	**George Washington** U.S. President	I have the Honor to inform Congress that a Reduction of the British Army under the Command of Lord Cornwallis is most happily effected. (Victory at Yorktown, 1781)
☐	***Thomas Paine** Political Writer	These are the times that try men's souls. [Some may] . . . shrink from the service of their country; but he that stands it *now* deserves the love and thanks of man and woman. (*The American Crisis*, December 1776)	☐	**Daniel Webster** Statesman	One country, one constitution, one destiny. (Speech, 1837)
☐	**Chief Seattle** Duwamish Leader	When the last red man shall have perished from the earth . . . these shores shall swarm with the invisible dead of my tribe . . . the dead are not . . . powerless. (Speech, 1854)	☐	**Daniel Webster** Statesman	Peaceable secession! Sir, your eyes and mine are never destined to see that miracle. (To the U.S. Senate, 1850)
☐	**William Tecumseh Sherman** Union General	If the people raise a great howl against my barbarity and cruelty, I will answer that war is war. If they . . . want peace, they must stop the war. (Letter prior to Sherman's March through Georgia, 1864)	☐	**Wendell Willkie** Politician	The only soil in which liberty can grow is that of a united people. We must have faith that the welfare of one is the welfare of all. (Speech, August 17, 1940)
☐	**Sitting Bull** Sioux Leader	Is it wicked for me because . . . I am a Sioux; because I was born where my father lived; because I would die for my people and my country? (Interview, 1891)	☐	**Woodrow Wilson** U.S. President	America cannot be an ostrich with its head in the sand. (Pre–World War I speech, 1916)
☐	***Elizabeth Cady Stanton** Women's Rights Leader	We hold these truths to be self-evident: that all men and women are created equal. (Declaration of Rights and Sentiments, 1848)		* Starred items might be most familiar to students	

Quotation Bingo Game Boards

Jesse Jackson 1941– Civil Rights Leader	**William Tecumseh Sherman** 1820–1891 Union General	**Oliver Wendell Holmes, Sr.** 1809–1894 Writer	**John Adams** 1735–1826 U.S. President	**Wendell Willkie** 1892–1944 Politician	**Frederick Douglass** 1817–1895 Abolitionist
Anne Hutchinson 1591–1643 Religious Leader	**ANY U.S. PRESIDENT**	**Harriet Tubman** 1820–1913 Abolitionist	**Jesse Jackson** 1941– Civil Rights Leader	**ANY U.S. PRESIDENT**	**Helen Keller** 1880–1968 Political Writer
Chief Seattle 1786–1866 Duwamish Leader	**Thomas Jefferson** 1743–1826 U.S. President	**Mother Jones** 1830–1930 Labor Reformer	**Chief Joseph** c.1841–1904 Nez Percé Leader	**Sojourner Truth** 1797–1883 Abolitionist	**Angelina Grimké** 1805–1879 Women's Rights Leader
Black Hawk 1767–1838 Sac Leader	**Nathan Hale** 1755–1776 Patriot	**Harriet Tubman** 1820–1913 Abolitionist	**Harriet Beecher Stowe** 1811–1896 Writer	**Thomas Paine** 1737–1809 Political Writer	**Daniel Webster** 1782–1852 Statesman
Jane Addams 1860–1935 Social Reformer	**ANY U.S. PRESIDENT**	**Emma Lazarus** 1849–1887 Writer and Poet	**Sitting Bull** c.1834–1890 Sioux Leader	**ANY U.S. PRESIDENT**	**Martin Luther King, Jr.** 1929–1968 Civil Rights Leader
Oliver Wendell Holmes, Sr. 1809–1894 Writer	**Elizabeth Cady Stanton** 1815–1902 Women's Rights Leader	**George Washington** 1732–1799 U.S. President	**Jane Addams** 1860–1935 Social Reformer	**Jimmy Carter** 1924– U.S. President	**Susan B. Anthony** 1820–1906 Women's Rights Leader
Abigail Adams 1774–1818 First Lady	**Samuel M. Jones** 1846–1904 Mayor of Toledo, OH Labor Reformer	**Abraham Lincoln** 1809–1865 U.S. President	**Benjamin Franklin** 1706–1790 Statesman	**Frederick Douglass** 1817–1895 Abolitionist	**Emma Lazarus** 1849–1887 Writer and Poet
Ida Tarbell 1857–1944 Writer and Social Reformer	**ANY U.S. PRESIDENT**	**Patrick Henry** 1736–1799 Patriot and Statesman	**Susan B. Anthony** 1820–1906 Women's Rights Leader	**ANY U.S. PRESIDENT**	**Ida Tarbell** 1857–1944 Writer and Social Reformer
Angelina Grimké 1805–1879 Women's Rights Leader	**Martin Luther King, Jr.** 1929–1968 Civil Rights Leader	**William Tecumseh Sherman** 1820–1891 Union General	**Sitting Bull** c.1834–1890 Sioux Leader	**John F. Kennedy** 1917–1963 U.S. President	**Anne Hutchinson** 1591–1643 Religious Leader

Quotation Bingo Game Boards

George Washington 1732–1799 Religious Leader	**Nathan Hale** 1755–1776 Patriot	**William Tecumseh Sherman** 1820–1891 Union General	**Emma Lazarus** 1849–1887 Writer and Poet	**Daniel Webster** 1782–1852 Statesman	**Martin Luther King, Jr.** 1929–1968 Civil Rights Leader
Daniel Webster 1782–1852 Statesman	ANY U.S. PRESIDENT	**Harriet Tubman** 1820–1913 Abolitionist	**Mother Jones** 1830–1930 Labor Reformer	ANY U.S. PRESIDENT	**Helen Keller** 1880–1968 Political Writer
Angelina Grimké 1805–1879 Women's Rights Leader	**Abigail Adams** 1774–1818 First Lady	**Chief Joseph** C.1841–1904 Nez Percé Leader	**John Adams** 1735–1826 U.S. President	**Benjamin Franklin** 1706–1790 Statesman	**Chief Seattle** 1786–1866 Duwamish Leader
Jesse Jackson 1941– Civil Rights Leader	**Thomas Jefferson** 1743–1826 U.S. President	**Frederick Douglass** 1817–1895 Abolitionist	**Chief Seattle** 1786–1866 Duwamish Leader	**Wendell Willkie** 1892–1944 Politician	**Ida Tarbell** 1857–1944 Writer and Social Reformer
Harriet Beecher Stowe 1811–1896 Writer	ANY U.S. PRESIDENT	**Samuel M. Jones** 1846–1904 Mayor of Toledo, OH Labor Reformer	**Abraham Lincoln** 1809–1865 U.S. President	ANY U.S. PRESIDENT	**Susan B. Anthony** 1820–1906 Women's Rights Leader
Black Hawk 1767–1838 Sac Leader	**Helen Keller** 1880–1968 Political Writer	**Thomas Paine** 1737–1809 Political Writer	**Black Hawk** 1767–1838 Sac Leader	**Harriet Beecher Stowe** 1811–1896 Writer	**Nathan Hale** 1755–1776 Patriot
Henry David Thoreau 1817–1862 Writer	**Abigail Adams** 1774–1818 First Lady	**Anne Hutchinson** 1591–1643 Religious Leader	**Benjamin Franklin** 1706–1790 Statesman	**Elizabeth Cady Stanton** 1815–1902 Women's Rights Leader	**Sojourner Truth** 1797–1883 Abolitionist
Sitting Bull 1834–1890 Sioux Leader	ANY U.S. PRESIDENT	**Woodrow Wilson** 1856–1924 U.S. President	**Patrick Henry** 1736–1799 Patriot and Statesman	ANY U.S. PRESIDENT	**Jane Addams** 1860–1935 Writer and Social Reformer
Elizabeth Cady Stanton 1815–1902 Women's Rights Leader	**Sojourner Truth** 1797–1883 Abolitionist	**Thomas Paine** 1737–1809 Political Writer	**Henry David Thoreau** 1817–1862 Writer	**John F. Kennedy** 1917–1963 U.S. President	**Chief Joseph** C.1841–1904 Nez Percé Leader

State Capital Map Search Game

⟡ Search the States for Historic Names ⟡

Players race to locate a state capital on a map using historic place names and other clues. Play one or two rounds for a quick time-filler or all 50 rounds for a State Capital marathon!

Materials

♛ detailed U.S. political and physical maps (one or two per player or pair)

♛ State Capital Map Search Clue Cards (pages 19–21)

♛ scrap paper

♛ (Optional) score sheet listing students' names, Place-Name Scavenger Hunt Glossary (page 24, for pregame or postgame scavenger hunt)

Players: any number of individuals or partners; a large group will also need a game monitor and a scorekeeper; see solitaire rules under "Variations"

Objective

Geographic Perspective (Diversity of People, Places, and Cultures; Location, Movement, and Connections): Using geographic historic clues and prior knowledge, locate places on a map of the United States.

Preparation

1. (Optional) Play the Place-Name Scavenger Hunt (pages 22–24). This works well as either a pregame warm-up to or a postgame review for the State Capital Map Search Game.

2. Copy and cut out the State Capital Map Search Game cards (pages 19–21).

3. Ask students to open their maps and have strips of scrap paper and pencil ready. They should write their names on each strip of paper. To estimate how many strips of paper students will need, multiply by 3 the number of rounds you wish to play (3 clues per round).

4. Assign a game monitor and a scorekeeper, if you are playing with a large group.

How to Play the Game (Group or Class Rules)

1 The game monitor draws a card and reads clue 3 (worth 3 points) aloud.

2 Players have about one minute to search their maps for the state capital that matches the clue. They write their answer and the number "3" on a slip of scrap paper and hand it to the score-keeper. (Note: The slips of paper already have students' names on them; see "Preparation.") There's no penalty for wrong answers, so encourage players to make educated guesses. Players can make one guess per clue.

3 When the answers have been collected, the game monitor reads clue 2 (worth 2 points). Again, students have one minute to write their answer and, this time, the number "2" on a piece of paper for the scorekeeper to collect. If players handed in a guess for clue 3 and want to stick with that answer, they don't have to fill out another slip of paper.

4 The game monitor reads clue 1 (worth 1 point) and students write down their final answer and the number "1" on a slip of paper. Again, if they have already turned in an answer they want to stick with, they don't have to fill out another slip for clue 1.

5 The game monitor states the answer. The scorekeeper puts all correct responses in a pile.

6 Play as many rounds as you like. After the game is over, the scorekeeper totals each player's score by counting the points on the correct answer slips.

Variations

Easier Game: Have students guess the state instead of the capital. Read the hints in parentheses after some of the clues.

Quick Time-Filler: Don't keep score. Just read each clue on a card and give students a short time to write down an answer and hold it in the air. Check the answers quickly after each clue is read and congratulate any winners. After the third clue, ask a winner to reveal the answer to the class.

Solitaire or Cooperative Version: Copy the cards and cut off the state capital and state name on each card. Challenge a student or cooperative group to place all 50 cards on a large U.S. map, by matching the clue cards to the correct state capital. (If a large map is unavailable, players can write the names of the states on the back of each card and arrange the cards alphabetically. They'll need a list of states to use as a reference.)

State Capital Map Search Game Clue Cards

Denver, Colorado

3 The western part was gained in the Mexican War and the eastern part was bought as part of the Louisiana Purchase.

2 The state name is Spanish for "reddish color."

1 A famous rocky peak is named for explorer Zebulon Pike.

Boise, Idaho

3 Lewis and Clark explored it along the Snake River. Mormons settled it.

2 Nez Percé National Park was named for a native people.

1 Many Coeur d'Alene people live in the state's northern part. Look for a town and lake of that name.

Baton Rouge, Louisiana

3 *Bayou*, a type of waterway, is a French version of a Choctaw word. (Tip: Look for bayous near rivers and lakes.)

2 The capital means "red baton" in French.

1 The state was named for a famous French king (Louis XIV).

Sacramento, California

3 Early Spanish settlers built missions, so many city names begin with *San* or *Santa* ("Saint").

2 This "Golden State" had a famous gold rush.

1 Eureka ("I have found it!" in Greek) is both the name of a city and the state motto.

Honolulu, Hawaii

3 Most place names in this state use only 12 letters: five vowels and *h, k, l, m, n, p,* and *w*.

2 In 1778, explorer Captain Cook called it "The Sandwich Islands."

1 Japan attacked Pearl Harbor on Oahu Island on December 7, 1941.

Frankfort, Kentucky

3 This former part of Virginia became a state in 1792, a decade after the Revolutionary War.

2 Many Scots-Irish immigrants settled in this state. Glasgow, for example, is named for a Scottish city.

1 A bomb-proof building in Fort Knox holds the nation's gold.

Little Rock, Arkansas

3 Part of the Louisiana Purchase, the eastern border of this state is the Mississippi River.

2 Ouachitas (Washitas) are a native people. (Tip: Look for a lake, river, and mountain with that name.)

1 President Bill Clinton grew up in a small town called Hope.

Atlanta, Georgia

3 This state name honors an English king (George II).

2 In 1864, Union troops burned a path from the capital to Savannah on the Atlantic coast.

1 Okefenokee (a swamp and a river) may mean "shaking Earth" in the Seminole language.

Topeka, Kansas

3 This prairie state name means "people of the wind" in a Sioux language.

2 Fort Leavenworth, now a city, protected pioneers on the Oregon Trail.

1 Dodge City was the end point of western cattle drives. From there, cattle were shipped by rail to the East.

Phoenix, Arizona

3 Fort Apache is named for a native people of the Southwest.

2 Because Mexico once owned the land, many cities have Spanish names: Mesa, Sierra Vista, Nogales.

1 The Yuma people lived in the southwest corner of the state. (Tip: Look for the city of Yuma.)

Tallahassee, Florida

3 Ponce de Leon named the lush state "flower feast" in Spanish.

2 Seminoles fought to keep this land—and won. (Tip: "Seminoles" is the nickname of what university?)

1 The state song is "Suwannee River," after a river that flows into the Gulf of Mexico.

Des Moines, Iowa

3 Herbert Hoover, a native of this state, was the first president born west of the Mississippi River.

2 Sioux City is named for several peoples who have a similar language.

1 French explorers named the capital city "from the monks" in French. A river shares the capital's name.

Juneau, Alaska

3 The state name means "what the sea breaks against" in the Aleut language. (Tip: Look for Aleutian Islands and a rugged coast.)

2 Seward persuaded the U.S. to buy the land from Russia. (Tip: A city and a peninsula are named for him.)

1 The capital is the last name of a gold miner.

Dover, Delaware

3 The state nickname is First State. It joined the Union in 1787.

2 The city of Wilmington was once a Swedish colony named Fort Christina.

1 The state is named for Lord De La Warr, who was a governor of the Virginia colony.

Indianapolis, Indiana

3 This state has a small but vital shore on Lake Michigan for shipping raw materials and goods to the East.

2 Tippecanoe (a river) may mean "buffalo fish" (Miami language).

1 This "land of Indians" has a "city of Indians" for a capital.

Montgomery, Alabama

3 The Choctawhatchee River is named for the Choctaw people.

2 Fort Mobile on the Gulf of Mexico was the state's first European settlement.

1 The cities of Selma and Birmingham are famous for civil rights protests in the 1960s.

Hartford, Connecticut

3 The state name (quinni-tukq-ut in Mohican) means "long river place." (Tip: The name refers to Long Island Sound.)

2 Many colonial city names end in the English suffix "bury."

1 Manchester and New London are also named after English cities.

Springfield, Illinois

3 Cattle were shipped east by way of the Great Lakes from this state's biggest city.

2 Joliet was a French explorer. (Tip: Look for the city of Joliet.)

1 Black Hawk defended his people's land along the Rock River. (Tip: Look for Rock Island, a city on the eastern border.)

State Capital Map Search Game Clue Cards

Jackson, Mississippi
3 This southern state's name means "Father of Waters."
2 The Natchez are a native people. (Tip: Look for a city and parkway.)
1 In the Yazoo Land Fraud, legislators sold much of the state to Georgia. (Tip: Look for the city of Yazoo and Yazoo River.)

Trenton, New Jersey
3 This former colony was once part of New York. (Tip: Look for English place names.)
2 Cities with "Orange" in their name were founded by Dutch traders in honor of a royal family.
1 Princeton was the nation's capital in 1783 and 1784.

Oklahoma City, Oklahoma
3 Native Americans were forced onto flat, dry, and barren reservations in this plains state.
2 The name of the state and capital means "red people" in Choctaw. (Tip: What capital and state share a name?)
1 Shawnee is a Native American place name.

St. Paul, Minnesota
3 The nickname of this northern state is "Land of 10,000 Lakes." It also borders a Great Lake (Superior).
2 The state name means "sky-tinted water" in a Sioux language.
1 The Mississippi River starts near Lake Itasca in the north central part of the state.

Concord, New Hampshire
3 This former colony was named for an English county.
2 The southeastern part of the state has English place names: Derry, Exeter, and Dover.
1 Lake Winnepesaukee (in the center) is a Native American place name.

Columbus, Ohio
3 The name of this mid-western state means "great river" in Iroquois. A great river of the same name forms its southern border.
2 A Great Lake forms most of the northern border.
1 The capital is named for a late 15th-century (1400s) explorer.

Lansing, Michigan
3 The state name means "great water" in Ojibwa (Chippewa).
2 Hurons are a native people. (Tip: Look for Port Huron, Lake Huron, and Huron River.)
1 Marquette, a Frenchman, explored this region. (Tip: Look for the city of Marquette in the north.)

Carson City, Nevada
3 The state name is Spanish for "snow-capped."
2 This desert state is largely deserted. It has few cities, and the U.S. government owns 85 percent of the land.
1 Gold seekers followed the Humboldt River past Winnemucca and Reno to the West.

Bismarck, North Dakota
3 This state takes half of its name from one of many Sioux divisions (Dakota).
2 Mandans are a native people. (Tip: Look for a city near the capital.)
1 Garrison Dam created Lake Sakakawea. Sacagawea, a Shoshone, guided explorers Lewis and Clark.

Boston, Massachusetts
3 This "Old Colony State" has English city names such as Worcester ("WOOS-ter") and Plymouth.
2 Minute Man National Park is between the cities of Concord and Lexington.
1 Salem was the site of 17th-century witchcraft trials.

Lincoln, Nebraska
3 This plains state means "flat water" in the Oto (Ute) language.
2 Fort Kearney, on the Platte River, protected and supplied pioneers on the Oregon Trail.
1 Omahas are a native people who lived in the eastern part of the state.

Raleigh, North Carolina
3 The capital is named for an Englishman (Sir Walter Raleigh) whose colony perished in 1587.
2 The first airplane flew at Kitty Hawk on the breezy coast. (Tip: Look for Wright Brothers National Monument.)
1 Many ships sank at Capes Fear and Lookout.

Annapolis, Maryland
3 This state near our nation's capital was named for Henrietta Maria, the wife of Charles I of England.
2 The state's northern border is the Mason-Dixon line, separating the North and the South.
1 In 1632, Lord Baltimore's brother established a colony in the Chesapeake area.

Helena, Montana
3 This western state's name comes from the Spanish word for "mountain."
2 Lewis Mountains, Lewistown, and Clark Fork River are named for two explorers.
1 General George Custer's infamous Battle of Little Bighorn took place in this state.

Albany, New York
3 In 1624, Henry Hudson explored the area for the Dutch. Fort Orange became the capital under a new name. (Tip: Hudson River.)
2 Oneontas are a native people. (Tip: Look for the city of Oneontas.)
1 The city of New Amsterdam now has an English name (New York).

Augusta, Maine
3 This New England state was governed by Massachusetts until 1820.
2 French explorers created place names such as Presque Isle ("almost island") and St. Croix ("Saint Cross"), especially in the north.
1 Penobscot River and Bay are named for a native people.

Jefferson City, Missouri
3 This state with many rivers means "town of big canoes."
2 The Pony Express started in St. Joseph.
1 The Oregon Trail began in Independence, later President Harry Truman's hometown.

Santa Fe, New Mexico
3 The capital is also the name of a western trail. (Tip: Atchison, Topeka, & ___ Railroad.)
2 This former Mexican land has many places with Spanish names: Las Cruces, Los Alamos, Rio Hondo.
1 Gallup is "The Indian Capital of America."

State Capital Map Search Game Clue Cards

Pierre, South Dakota
3 The state is named for a Sioux people. The capital has a French name.

2 Discovery of gold in the Black Hills led to battles between the United States Army and native peoples.

1 Wounded Knee near the Bad Lands is the site of a bloody massacre of Native Americans.

Richmond, Virginia
3 This "Mother of Presidents" state gave the nation eight presidents (as of 2000).

2 Early settlers named cities after English cities: Norfolk, Hampton, and Suffolk.

1 Elizabeth I of England was the "Virgin Queen." This state honors her nickname.

Columbia, South Carolina
3 A 1562 French colony on Parris Island failed.

2 The biggest port (Charleston) was named for Charles I of England. The early colony grew food for slaves in the West Indies.

1 The Civil War began at Fort Sumter. (Tip: Look for the city of Sumter.)

Montpelier, Vermont
3 The name of this New England state is French for "Green Mountain."

2 The capital has a French name, too, but cities such as Essex have English names.

1 Bratleboro used to be called Fort Dummer, a British outpost.

Cheyenne, Wyoming
3 The capital is named for a native people of the western plains.

2 The state name means "mountains and valleys alternating" (Lenape or Delaware language). The Grand Tetons are major mountains in the western part of the state.

1 Yellowstone was the first national park in the United States.

Providence, Rhode Island
3 This eastern state was named after a Greek island (Rhodes).

2 Pawtuckets are a native people. (Tip: Look for a city.)

1 Roger Williams, exiled by Puritans, founded the future capital and gave it a religious name.

Salt Lake City, Utah
3 The state name means "people of the mountains" in Ute.

2 Mormons led by Brigham Young settled the state. Many Mormons still live there today.

1 The area was once a big sea that dried up long ago, leaving salty lakes behind.

Madison, Wisconsin
3 The capital is also the name of an early U.S. president, but the area became a state a few decades after his term.

2 French trappers reached what is now nicknamed the "Badger State" by way of the Great Lakes.

1 Eau Claire, a city, means "clear water" in French.

Harrisburg, Pennsylvania
3 The biggest city (Philadelphia) was the nation's capital in 1776.

2 Gettysburg is the site of a bloody Civil War battle.

1 William Penn, an English Quaker, was granted the land in 1681 and gave it its name.

Austin, Texas
3 The state name is Native American ("friends"), but many place names are Spanish: Del Rio, El Paso, Laredo.

2 In the 1800s, cattle trails led north to Kansas.

1 Sam Houston was its president before it became a state.

Charleston, West Virginia
3 This "Mountain State" was part of another state that shares part of its name.

2 Morgan founded the first permanent settlement in 1731. (Tip: Look for the city of Morgantown.)

1 The capital was named for Charles I of England.

Salem, Oregon
3 This coastal state lent its name to a famous pioneer trail.

2 The Columbia River is named for a ship whose captain claimed the land for the United States.

1 Millionaire John Jacob Astor's fur depot is now the city of Astoria.

Nashville, Tennessee
3 The state name is a Cherokee word, but the meaning isn't clear.

2 The state was briefly named Franklin, now a city near today's capital.

1 Many cities end in the English and French suffix *ville*: Crossville, Shelbyville, Knoxville, and Maryville.

Olympia, Washington
3 The name of this coastal state honors a famous U.S. president.

2 The biggest city (Seattle) is the name of a famous Duwamish leader.

1 Lewis and Clark explored the Columbia River on the southern border of the state.

Place-Name Scavenger Hunt

❧ Cultural Exploration and Settlement ❧

Student teams discover patterns of exploration, movement, and settlement by classifying and locating cultural place-names on a map of the U.S.

Materials

Players: any number

- Place-Name Scavenger Hunt Glossary (page 24)
- photocopy of a U.S. map
- index to the map, a mapping software program, or access to a searchable online map
- U.S. atlas with an index
- (Optional) Internet access, map of England (extension), map of former Native American lands (extension)

Objective

Geographic Perspective (Location, Movement, and Connections): Identify and analyze patterns of movement of people who have contributed to the American heritage, including settlers, Native Americans, explorers, and others.

Math: Plot patterns of movement on a map.

Language Arts: Identify the origins of words adopted from the Spanish and French languages.

Preparation

1. Divide the class into four groups: French, Spanish, English, and Native American. Identify any French- or Spanish-speaking students as experts for these groups to consult.

2. Supply groups with a photocopy of a U.S. map or a desk map on which they can write. Make sure each group also has access to either an index for the map, a software program with a searchable U.S. map, or a Web site with a searchable map of the U.S. (See "Web Links.")

3. Photocopy the Place-Name Glossary (page 24). Cut apart the four Place-Name lists, and give

each group its list of names. Discuss: What type of geographic features have place-names? (*cities, towns, rivers, lakes, bays, capes, mountains, plains, and so on*) Point out that many Spanish names include the articles *la, el,* and *los* ("the") or the preposition *de* ("of"). Many French names include *la, le,* and *les* ("the") and the prepositions *de* ("of") and *du* ("of the").

✦ Review how to use a geographic index or a computer search engine.

How to Play the Game

✦ Teams work cooperatively to locate and plot on a U.S. map the place-names on their list. Many names apply to more than one place; students need only find one example per name.

✦ After students have located and marked at least 20 place-names, copy and discuss their place-name maps with the class. Ask: What patterns do you see? Do you notice anything odd or unusual? Based on the data, what regions did Spanish people explore? (*Florida, Southwest, Nevada, Colorado, California*) French people? (*northeast border with Canada, Great Lakes, Louisiana and parts of the Mississippi River valley*) English people? (*all regions, with concentrations of names in New England*) Where did Native Americans live? (*all over, except Hawaii, which was first settled by Polynesian peoples*)

Extensions

Explorer Place-Names: Using a list of explorers and other leaders from your history textbook, have students use place-names to determine roughly where these people explored. For example, there are many places named after the explorers Marquette, Joliet, Lewis and Clark, Champlain, Hudson, and so on.

Great Britain Scavenger Hunt: Have students locate the English place-names (page 24) on a map of Great Britain. What other English cities or rivers have counterparts in the U.S.?

Native American Scavenger Hunt: Using a map of Native American lands (commonly available in history textbooks) or the Internet (see "Web Links"), challenge students to look for other place names in that category. Native American names tend to be spelled phonetically. Also, students can use an almanac or a dictionary to determine which states have Native American names. (Note: Some state name origins are listed as clues in the State Capital Map Search Game cards on pages 19–21.)

First Nations/First Peoples: www.dickshovel.com/www.html
Extensive online encyclopedia of Native American peoples. Click on "Compact History: Geographic Overview" for a geographic list of groups. Also see www.nativeweb.org.

Mapquest: www.mapquest.com
Online maps searchable by city and state, but not by physical features such as rivers. For example, entering "Choctaw" for "city" and "United States" for "country" yields ten maps of U.S. cities by that name.

Place-Name Scavenger Hunt Glossary

🏁 French Place-Names 🏁

Find these French words on a U.S. map.
In what regions are French words common?

Baie: Bay
Bas or *Basse*: Low
Bayou: Waterway
Beau or *Belle*: Beautiful
Blanc or *Blanche*: White
Bon or *Bonne*: Good
Cap: Cape
Château: Castle
Croix: Cross
Crosse: Cross
Fond: Bottom
Grand or *Grande*: Great
Gros or *Grosse*: Big
Haut or *Haute*: High
Isle: Island
Lac: Lake

Mont: Mountain
Petit or *Petite*: Small
Plat or *Platte*: Flat
Prairie: Prairie
Rivière: River
Roche: Rock
Rouge: Red
Royal or *Royale*: Royal
Saint or *Sainte*: Saint
Terre: Land
Trois: Three
Ville: Town or City

🏁 Spanish Place-Names 🏁

Find these Spanish words on a U.S. map.
In what regions are Spanish words common?

Agua: Water
Alta: High
Amarillo: Yellow
Bahía: Bay
Bajo or *Baja*: Low
Blanco or *Blanca*: White
Bueno or *Buena*: Good
Ciudad: City
Cruz: Cross
Diablo: Devil
Dorado: Gold
Grande: Big
Isla: Island
Madre: Mother
Nuevo or *Nueva*: New
Padre: Father

Paso: Pass, Way Through
Piedra: Stone
Pueblo: Town
Puerto: Port
Rio: River
San or *Santa*: Saint
Sierra: Jagged Peaks
Tierra: Land
Vegas: Plains
Viejo or *Vieja*: Old
Villa: Town
Vista: View

🏁 Native American Names 🏁

Find the names of these Native American peoples on a U.S. map. Where did each group live?

Apache
Arapaho
Athabascan
Blackfoot
Cherokee
Cheyenne
Chickasaw
Chippewa
Choctaw
Comanche
Dakota
Hopi
Huron
Iroquois
Mandan
Maumee
Miami
Missouri

Mohawk
Narragansett
Navajo
Natchez
Nez Percé
Omaha
Osage
Ouachita
Paiute
Pamunkey
Penobscot
Potawatomi
Pueblo
Shawnee
Shoshone
Sioux
Ute
Winnebago

🏁 English Place-Names 🏁

Find the names of these British cities on a U.S. map. Where did Britons explore and settle?

Aberdeen
Andover
Birmingham
Boston
Brighton
Bristol
Cambridge
Cheltenham
Dartmouth
Dover
Exeter
Falmouth
Flint
Gloucester
Hamilton
Hastings
Ipswich
Lancaster

Milford
Newark
Newcastle
Newport
Northampton
Norwich
Oxford
Plymouth
Portland
Portsmouth
Reading
Salisbury
Southampton
Stockton
Winchester
Woodstock
Worcester
York

Passport to America Game

☙ An Immigration Detective Game ☙

Players draw from a set of "passports," developed from biographies of actual U.S. immigrants. By asking each other yes-or-no questions, they deduce six facts about their opponent's immigrant (country of origin, language, century of immigration, U.S. state of settlement, occupation, and reason for immigrating).

Materials

Players: 2 individuals or 2 pairs

- 🛡 Passport to America Game Data Bank (page 28)
- 🛡 Passport to America Game Passports (pages 29–34)
- 🛡 (Optional) World and U.S. maps

Objectives

Geographic Perspective (Diversity of Peoples, Places, and Cultures; Global Issues and Events): Use biographical information to identify patterns of and motivations for immigration.

Math: Use logical thinking skills to classify information (by asking yes-or-no questions).

Language Arts: Formulate questions for an interview (extension).

Preparation

1. Copy and cut out the immigration passports (pages 29–34) on the solid lines (four passports per page). Fold each passport accordion-style on the dotted lines so that the "U.S. Passport" emblem is on the cover and the quotation is on the back.

2. Each player needs a copy of the Immigration Data Bank (page 28) and an immigrant's passport, chosen at random. Instruct players to read their passports to themselves and to keep the information hidden from their opponent.

3. Review how to ask a yes-or-no question. Examples of a legal and an illegal question are at the top of the Immigration Data Bank form.

How to Play the Game

1. Players take turns asking each other yes-or-no questions about any one of the six categories of facts on their opponent's passport. Players must answer all questions truthfully.

2. All the facts on the passports are included on the Immigration Data Bank form. Once a player has ruled out a fact, such as a country or a language, he or she should cross it out. Once a player has identified a fact, he or she should circle it and write it in the blank next to each category name.

3. The first player to guess all six facts about their opponent's immigrant wins.

4. Time permitting, players can each draw a new passport and a blank Data Bank form and play again. They should take turns asking the first question of each game.

Variations

Discuss Strategies: Students can learn from each other as they share questioning strategies that helped them locate answers. Ask: What strategies for winning can you share with the class? After just one game, students learn to ask questions that eliminate more than one fact at a time. Example: "Does your immigrant come from Asia?" instead of "Does your immigrant come from China?" A "yes" answer to the broader question rules out all countries that are not in Asia; a "no" answer rules out all countries that are in Asia. Once students have deduced a fact, they can often use that information to pinpoint or narrow down other facts. For example, if they discover that the immigrant's country is Ireland, then they know the language must be English (since Gaelic is not on the Data Bank form). Also, they can surmise that the immigrant might have arrived during a wave of Irish immigration, such as after the potato famine (19th century).

Easier and Faster Game: Limit the fact categories to "Country," "Language," and "U.S. State." Instruct students to announce the name of their immigrant at the beginning of the game. The name can sometimes help players identify the world region, country, and language more quickly.

Extensions

Interview Questions: Tell students to pretend they are newspaper reporters whose job is to interview one of the immigrants. To prepare, they should read the selected immigrant's "passport" and research related facts such as the country of origin. Their goal is to generate a list of ten questions written to reveal interesting details about the immigrant's life. A rule of thumb is to avoid questions that are answered simply "yes" or "no." Provide examples of specific questions such as, "Why was your country at war?" "What was the first thing you did when you set foot on American soil?" "How are Americans different from the people in your country?"

More Passports: The "Book Links" and "Web Links" are sources of oral histories and primary-source documents about immigrants. Students can use these and other resources to create passports similar to those in the game. An easy approach is to create passports of famous immigrants such as Alexander Graham Bell, Elizabeth Blackwell, Andrew Carnegie, Albert Einstein, Marcus Garvey, Emma Goldman, Alexander Hamilton, Al Jolson, John Paul Jones, Mother Jones, Golda Meir, Levi Strauss, and so on.

★ ☆
★ ★

Angel Island: www.aiisf.org/ai/index.html
The entry point for Asian immigrants. See also www.angelisland.org

Ellis Island Immigration Museum: www.ellisisland.org/
Immigrant Wall of Honor with 500,000 names, History Center with access to immigrant records and genealogy information (including celebrities), brief audio interviews with immigrants in WAV format.

Library of Congress: American Life Histories Collection:
rs6.loc.gov/ammem/ndlpedu/lessons/oralhist/ohhome.html
Lessons for searching and using primary source materials, including oral histories of immigrants. Search by topic (history, geography, politics, social science, and so on), historic period (1400s to present), or geographical region.

National Museum of American Jewish History: www.nmajh.org/
Information about Jewish immigrants.

PBS's *Ancestors*: www2.kbyu.byu.edu/ancestors
Family history and genealogy information, a 7th–12th-grade teacher's guide, and a resource list to accompany a ten-part video series. Companion book is *Ancestors: A Beginner's Guide to Family History and Genealogy.*

U.S. Committee for Refugees (USCR): www.refugees.org/fieldmain.htm
Photos, news, publications, links, and RealAudio clips of personal experiences related by contemporary refugees from Sudan, Iraq, Bosnia, Rwanda, and other war-torn countries. For more information, write to USCR, 1717 Massachusetts Ave. NW, Washington, DC 20036; 202/347-3507.

U.S. Immigration and Naturalization Service (INS): www.ins.usdoj.gov
Laws, information, forms that students can practice filling out, and an online practice test for the U.S. history portion of the exam.

U.S. State Department: www.state.gov
Click on "K–12 Students: Enter web site here" in the upper left corner of the main page for social studies and geographical information; background on what the state department has done in the past and is doing now regarding foreign relations; and more reference material.

BOOK LINKS

American Mosaic: The Immigrant Experience in the Words of Those Who Lived It by Joan Morrison and Charlotte Fox Zabusky (Dutton, 1980).

Immigrant Kids by Russell Freedman (Dutton, 1980). Extraordinary photos and stories of ordinary children make for great student reading about the immigrant experience. Also check out Freedman's other books on children in the west, cowboys, and child laborers.

Immigrant Women edited by Maxine Schwartz Seller (State University of New York Press, 1994). Includes primary document accounts by immigrants.

Island of Hope, Island of Tears by David M. Brownstone et al. (Rawson, Wade, 1979). Immigrants who passed through Ellis Island tell their stories.

New Americans: An Oral History by Al Santoli (Viking, 1988). The stories of contemporary immigrants from a variety of social and economic classes and countries of origin.

Passport to America Game Data Bank

DIRECTIONS:

Take turns asking yes-or-no questions about one another's immigrant.

Illegal Question: Where is your immigrant from?

Legal Question: Is your immigrant from Asia?

Cross out items below as you rule them out. Circle or write one fact in each category as you discover information about your opponent's immigrant.

The first player to discover all six facts is the winner.

★ ★

1. Country: _____

AMERICAS
Barbados   Canada   Cuba   Haiti
Mexico

ASIA
Armenia   China   Japan   Vietnam

EUROPE
Bosnia   England   Germany   Ireland
Italy   Lithuania   Norway   Poland
Spain   Switzerland   Ukraine

2. Language: _____

Armenian   Lithuanian
Bosnian   Norwegian
Chinese   Polish
English   Russian
French   Spanish
German   Ukrainian
Italian   Vietnamese
Japanese

★ ★

3. State: _____

EAST
Florida   Maryland   Massachusetts
New York   Pennsylvania   Rhode Island

CENTRAL
Illinois   Louisiana   Minnesota
Ohio

WEST
Arizona   California   New Mexico
Washington

4. Job: _____

Business owner   Homemaker
Clergy or religious   Laborer
leader   Professional
Factory worker   Service worker
Farmer   Student
Government worker

★ ★

5. Century: _____

15th (1400s)   18th (1700s)
16th (1500s)   19th (1800s)
17th (1600s)   20th (1900s)

6. Reason: _____

Economic gain   Poverty
Political freedom   War
Religious freedom

★ ★

OFFICIAL PASSPORT

The United States of America

Edward

was ten years old when his family sailed from Italy to the New World. As an adult, he became the U.S. Commissioner (head) of Immigration.

EDWARD CORSI

Country: Italy, Europe
Language: Italian
Century: 20th (1907)
U.S. State: New York, New York (Ellis Island)
Job: Government worker
Reason to Immigrate: Economic gain

The steamer had weathered one of the worst storms in our captain's memory. Glad we were to leave the open sea. We looked with wonder on this miraculous land of our dreams. Jabbered conversation, sharp cries, laughs and cheers. . . . Mothers and fathers lifted up babies so that they, too, could see the Statue of Liberty.

—Edward Corsi

OFFICIAL PASSPORT

The Colonies of America

Prince

was a free black man who fought as a patriot in the Battle of Bunker Hill in the American Revolution. He was also a successful businessman and active in colonial government.

PRINCE HALL

Country: Barbados, Americas
Language: English
Century: 18th (1765)
U.S. State: Boston, Massachusetts
Job: Business owner (various businesses)
Reason to Immigrate: Poverty

Prince Hall urged the General Court of Massachusetts "to abolish the traffic in human beings," a plea to end slavery. The court complied, passing an act to prohibit the slave trade in Massachusetts colony a century before the U.S. Civil War.

OFFICIAL PASSPORT

The United States of America

Victor

grew up very poor, but worked three jobs in the U.S. to buy a house. While cleaning a floor, he found $600. No one claimed the cash, so Victor donated it to help a sick child.

VICTOR BACELIS

Country: Mexico, Americas
Language: Spanish
Century: 20th (1990s)
U.S. State: Fremont, California
Job: Service Worker (fast food)
Reason to Immigrate: Poverty

When I was growing up, the most important thing to my parents was to be clean and honest. . . . Life has been nice to me. I can work. I'm healthy. I have what I need to live.

—Victor Bacelis, to the *San Jose Mercury News*

OFFICIAL PASSPORT

The United States of America

Mila

joined her children and grandchildren in the U.S. At age 65, she learned English by trading favorite recipes with other immigrants. Together, they published a cookbook.

MILA ORKIS

Country: Ukraine, Europe
Language: Ukrainian
Century: 20th (1990s)
U.S. State: San Jose, California
Job: Homemaker
Reason to Immigrate: Religious freedom (Jewish)

In 1991, the Soviet Union broke into several nations. Food and goods became scarce, and so buyers had to stand in long lines.

Plenty of food here and no lines! I very much like America! I would kneel on the ground to thank America for helping Jews from Russia!

—Mila Orkis, to Knight-Ridder Newspapers

OFFICIAL PASSPORT

The United States of America

Alexander, his family, and seven friends floated on the Caribbean Sea for five days on a crowded, homemade raft to escape Cuba and start a life in the U.S.

ALEXANDER SANTOS

Country: Cuba, Americas
Language: Spanish
Century: 20th (1992)
U.S. State: Miami, Florida
Job: Student
Reason to Immigrate: Political freedom (communism)

Alexander's father is a woodworker. His mother is a nurse. In Cuba, Alexander would have been a train mechanic. In the U.S., he is learning English so that he can go to college.

I came here to have a future.
—Alexander Santos, to Knight-Ridder Newspapers

OFFICIAL PASSPORT

The United States of America

Pauline worked long hours at the Triangle Shirtwaist Factory as a child. The factory burned in 1911, killing 146 workers due to unsafe conditions. Pauline became a labor leader.

PAULINE NEWMAN

Country: Lithuania, Europe
Language: Lithuanian
Century: 20th (1901)
U.S. State: New York, New York (Ellis Island)
Job: Factory worker (textiles)
Reason to Immigrate: Religious freedom (Jewish)

Pauline helped organize a garment union and led a strike to improve working conditions of immigrants.

Conditions were dreadful in those days, but we believed in what we were doing. We fought and we bled and we died.

—Pauline Newman, from *American Mosaic*

OFFICIAL PASSPORT

The United States of America

John and his family were forced from their home by Turks, who later massacred many Armenians. They ate wild grass and bread in the Arabian desert and lived in caves to survive.

JOHN DAROUBIAN

Country: Armenia, Asia
Language: Armenian
Century: 20th (1919)
U.S. State: New York, New York (Ellis Island)
Job: Business owner (importer/retailer)
Reason to Immigrate: War (Turkish massacre of Armenians)

We were lucky. Other Armenians saw their whole families shot, stabbed, clubbed to death. We were dreaming of America. Many of our people were sent back. In New York, the first thing I said was, "School. I must be in school." At age 16, I went to school at night and worked during the day.

—John Daroubian, from *American Mosaic*

OFFICIAL PASSPORT

The United States of America

Taro was imprisoned in a U.S. camp from December 7, 1941, the day Japan attacked Pearl Harbor, until 1946, the year after World War II ended. He and his wife lost their business.

TARO MURATA

Country: Japan, Asia
Language: Japanese
Century: 20th (1907)
U.S. State: Seattle, Washington
Job: Business owner (dry cleaning)
Reason to Immigrate: Economic gain

I worked long hours on that business. We saved enough money to educate our children at the university. My son couldn't get hired to build aircraft because he was Japanese. There was a lot of suspicion in those days. He got a job in Japan. He can't come back since he fought on the other side.

—Taro Murata, from *American Mosaic*

OFFICIAL PASSPORT

The United States of America

Isabella

worked from childhood to old age picking apples, grapes, peaches, olives and prunes. She never learned to read and write, but learned a lot traveling all over the U.S.

ISABELLA MENDOZA

Country: Mexico, North America
Language: Spanish
Century: 20th (1915)
U.S. State: Santa Cruz, California
Job: Laborer (migrant farm worker)
Reason to Immigrate: Poverty

I was 15 when I had the first child. My children worked in the fields before they started school. We was always going from one place to another. You'd sleep in the car or camp in the dark. I know this whole country like a book. You don't get ahead. The money looks good, but it would creep away.
—Isabella Mendoza, from American Mosaic

OFFICIAL PASSPORT

The United States of America

Tanya

survived a Jewish ghetto and German concentration camp in World War II (1939-1945). Her mother, daughter, six siblings, nieces, nephews— her whole family died.

TANYA SHIMIEWSKY

Country: Poland, Europe
Language: Polish
Century: 20th (1950)
U.S. State: Chicago, Illinois
Job: Business owner (rooming house)
Reason to Immigrate: Religious freedom (Jewish)

Lodz was a closed ghetto. There was barbed wire. The Germans took out people [to camps]. One day all the old people. Another day, the children. In only one camp they kept children alive. Then they took us out. They took our clothes, cut off our hair. We lived in shacks, no heat. So little food.
—Tanya Shimiewsky, from American Mosaic

OFFICIAL PASSPORT

The United States of America

Hoa

was a rich Vietnamese government official who advised American officials. He lost everything when the U.S. pulled out of Vietnam. After barely escaping, he moved to a poor neighborhood in Ohio.

HOA TRAN

Country: Vietnam, Asia
Language: Vietnamese
Century: 20th (1975)
U.S. State: Columbus, Ohio
Job: Service worker (waiter)
Reason to Immigrate: War (U.S. evacuation from Saigon as the Vietnam War ended)

I worked in a warehouse— heavy work, nighttime. Then I worked as a waiter. I'm studying accounting. I have friends who are very unhappy. They had high positions; now they're delivering milk, working in a factory. We live very poor, but we accept it. I accept everything that fate gave to me. —Hoa Tran, from American Mosaic

---

OFFICIAL PASSPORT

The United States of America

Guri

lost her husband, two sons, her home, and much of her livestock in a conflict with Native Americans. She stayed to rebuild her farm, helping all of her daughters settle as well.

GURI ENDRESON

Country: Norway, Europe
Language: Norwegian
Century: 19th (1856)
U.S. State: A homestead in Minnesota
Job: Farmer
Reason to Immigrate: Economic gain

I escaped with my life, and four daughters also came through the danger. Daughters Guri and Britha were carried off, but fled and got away alive. On the third day, Americans found them on the prairie. I hovered between fear and hope and almost crazy . . . God be thanked, I kept my life and my sanity.
—Guri Endreson, letter to Norway

OFFICIAL PASSPORT

The United States of America

Philippe

was eight years old when his family left their farm in Quebec to work in the textile mills of New England. After 60 years in the mills, he was forced to quit because of illness.

PHILIPPE LEMAY

Country: Canada, Americas
Language: French
Century: 19th (1864)
U.S. State: Lowell, Massachusetts
Job: Factory worker (textiles)
Reason to Immigrate: Poverty

The pay was fifty cents a day and the board cost two dollars a week. The workday began at five o'clock and finished at eight o'clock at night, every day. It was good to have a steady job and pay. We wanted to better our condition. Out of wages we built churches and schools.

—Philippe Lemay,
The French Canadian Textile Worker

OFFICIAL PASSPORT

The United States of America

Albert

couldn't speak a word of English at first, but he learned. Relatives hired him to sell dry goods and groceries to miners and farmers in Spanish-American towns.

ALBERT ZEIGLER

Country: Germany, Europe
Language: German
Century: 19th (1884)
U.S. State: Socorro, New Mexico
Job: Business owner (general store)
Reason to Immigrate: Economic gain

My brother Jake made trips to peddle goods. We had a wagon and good horses. The country in those days was not safe. Once a masked bandit stepped up to the wagon and drew a gun. Jake and the driver were too slow, and the bandit shot at them. Jake did not make many more sales trips.

—Albert Zeigler,
Pioneer Story

OFFICIAL PASSPORT

The United States of America

Heinrich

first tried farming for a few years in the Midwest. Then, in 1846, he and four other immigrants set off to mine California gold at Sutter's fort. He later returned to his homeland.

HEINRICH LIENHARD

Country: Switzerland, Europe
Language: German
Century: 19th (1843)
U.S. State: Sutter's Fort, California
Job: Laborer (miner)
Reason to Immigrate: Economic gain

The discovery of gold at Sutter's fort triggered a rush of immigrants. Lienhard described the effects on Johann Sutter and his family in a diary.

The great rush arrived at the fort. My cook left me, like everyone else. The merchants, doctors, lawyers, sea captains all left their wives and families.

—Johann (John) Sutter

OFFICIAL PASSPORT

The United States of America

Mina

witnessed the Serbian assault on her hometown of Sarajevo. She and her family fled for refugee camps in Croatia and Slovenia. Then Mina won a scholarship to the U.S.

MINA KOVACEVIC

Country: Bosnia, Europe
Language: Bosnian (formerly Serbo-Croatian)
Century: 20th (1993)
U.S. State: Pittsburgh, Pennsylvania
Job: Professional (psychologist)
Reason to Immigrate: War

Our car was stopped by Serb soldiers. They told us we were being held as hostages. The soldiers made lists of children, threatening to kill them. Along with other men, my father was searched. The soldiers began forcing the men into a truck. I begged and convinced the commander to let my dad go.

—Mina Kovacevic,
U.S.C.R. interview

OFFICIAL PASSPORT

The Colonies of America

William sailed to America on the famous *Mayflower* and helped to establish Plymouth Plantation. He had not farmed since age 17 and, like other Pilgrims, had much to learn to survive.

WILLIAM BRADFORD

Country: England, Europe
Language: English
Century: 17th (1620)
U.S. State: Plymouth, Massachusetts
Job: Government worker (governor)
Reason to Immigrate: Religious freedom (Separatist)

In these hard and difficult beginnings they found some discontents . . . but they were soon quelled . . . by the wisdom, patience, and just and equal carriage of things. . . . That which was most sad . . . was that in two or three months the half of their company died . . . some times two or three of a day.
—William Bradford, *History of Plymouth Plantation*

OFFICIAL PASSPORT

The Colonies of America

Francisco helped to establish a fort (now the oldest European city in America) to prevent French settlers from claiming Florida.

FRANCISCO GRAJALES

Country: Spain, Europe
Language: Spanish
Century: 16th (1565)
U.S. State: St. Augustine, Florida
Job: Clergyman (chaplain)
Reason to Immigrate: Economic gain

Our fort is at a distance of about fifteen leagues from that of the enemy. The energy and talents of two brave captains . . . and their brave soldiers, who had no tools with which to work the earth, accomplished the construction of this fortress of defense."
—Francisco Grajales

OFFICIAL PASSPORT

The Colonies of America

Anne first settled among the Puritans at Plymouth Colony, but was banished for holding religious meetings, especially for women. She founded a settlement in Rhode Island.

ANNE HUTCHINSON

Country: England, Europe
Language: English
Century: 17th (1634)
U.S. State: Providence, Rhode Island
Job: Clergywoman
Reason to Immigrate: Religious freedom

The Puritan clergy of Massachusetts found Anne Hutchinson guilty of having "troubled the peace of the commonwealth [through actions] not fitting for [a woman]."

OFFICIAL PASSPORT

The United States of America

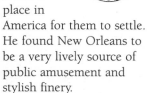

Henry was chosen by several English families to locate a place in America for them to settle. He found New Orleans to be a very lively source of public amusement and stylish finery.

HENRY FEARON

Country: England, Europe
Language: English
Century: 19th (1818)
U.S. State: New Orleans, Louisiana
Job: Professional (surgeon)
Reason to Immigrate: Economic gain

French language is still predominant . . . I was not a little surprised to find . . . the markets, shops, theatre, circus, and public ballrooms open. Gambling houses throng the city: all coffeehouses . . . are occupied from morning until night . . . The general style of living is luxurious. Houses are elegantly furnished. —Henry Fearon

OFFICIAL PASSPORT
The United States of America

Margaret Ann
left Ireland to join her husband, Jeremiah, in America. She needed a letter of reference, attesting to her character, to enter the country. The McCartys raised four children.

MARGARET ANN McCARTY
....
Country: Ireland, Europe
Language: English
Century: 19th (1852)
U.S. State: Carrollton, New York
Job: Homemaker
Reason to Immigrate: Poverty (potato famine)

Bearer is the lawful wife of the above named Jeremiah McCarty. She is about [to emigrate] to America to join her husband. She is an honest, virtuous, well-conducted woman.

—John Sheehan, Parish Priest, in a letter of reference for Margaret Ann McCarty

OFFICIAL PASSPORT
The United States of America

Roberta,
at age five, entered America with her mother via Angel Island, an immigration center that was overcrowded, unclean, and a fire hazard.

ROBERTA YEE
....
Country: China, Asia
Language: Chinese
Century: 20th (1930)
U.S. State: Palo Alto, California
Job: Professional (real estate agent)
Reason to Immigrate: Poverty

I grew up in Locke [a Chinatown]. When someone won the lottery . . . the kids would run to find the winner, hoping he'd give us some-thing . . . . My father had been a landowner in China, but [here he] sprayed trees and picked fruit . . . . His investment was us kids; that's what it was all about.

—Roberta Yee, to *Smithsonian* magazine

OFFICIAL PASSPORT
The United States of America

Tin-Wo
was a cook for Chinese immigrants who were building railroad tracks. He learned English, started a business, and became the first Chinese person to vote in his county.

CHAN TIN-WO
....
Country: China, Asia
Language: Chinese
Century: 19th (1860s)
U.S. State: Tucson, Arizona
Job: Business owner (grocery store)
Reason to Immigrate: Economic gain

[He] is the most prosperous groceryman in this city. Chan is a Republican striker and may be said to be on the wrong side of the fence, but he has a reputation of being about as honest and square in his dealing as men are generally made.

—The Arizona Daily Star

OFFICIAL PASSPORT
The Colonies of America

Jean Baptiste
was born to a slave mother and a pirate father. He first moved to New Orleans and then Illinois with his wife Kittihawa and two children.

JEAN BAPTISTE POINT DU SABLE
....
Country: Haiti, Americas
Language: French
Century: 18th (1765)
U.S. State: Chicago, Illinois
Job: Business owner (fur trader)
Reason to Immigrate: Economic gain

Jean Baptiste is known as "the authenticated father of the nation's second largest city—Chicago." His initial trading post there had a mill, bakery, dairy, smokehouse (for meat), workshop, horse stable, barn, and other structures. Jean Baptiste spoke French, Spanish, English, and several Native American dialects, and collected art.

CHAPTER 2

Colonial America

Courageous Colony

❧ A Colonial Survival Board Game ❧

Players begin the game as indentured servants and work their way up to gentry status by answering questions about early colonial life in Virginia.

Materials

Players: 2 to 4 players

🛡 Courageous Colony game board (poster included with this book)

🛡 Courageous Colony Cards (pages 37 and 38)

🛡 playing pieces (one per player)

Objectives

Historical Perspective (Comprehending the Past): Identify and understand the people and events that shaped early American colonial history.

Geographic Perspective (People, Places, and Cultures; Human/Environment Interaction): Reconstruct the past by experiencing the pitfalls and successes that affected Jamestown colonists. Understand how colonists interacted with the environment and Native American peoples.

Preparation

⚝ Laminate the game board (poster).

⚝ Copy and cut out the cards (pages 37 and 38).

⚝ Locate one playing piece per player, such as playing pieces from old board games, thimbles, miniature toy figures, dried pasta, and so on.

How to Play the Game

Rules for playing are provided on the game board. Point out to students that 1) the answers to the Examination Card questions are italicized, and 2) the footnotes provide additional information and should not be read until the answers are revealed.

Extensions

Internet Research: The Internet is rich with material for students about early colonial life. (See "Web Links.")

Carol Hurst's Children's Literature Site:
www.carolhurst.com/newsletters/newsletters11a.html
Volume 1, Number 1 (April 1996) of her online newspaper has an extensive list of recommended books for children about colonial America, including fiction and nonfiction. Also includes classroom project suggestions and links.

Colonial American History Resources: www.bham.wednet.edu/colonial.htm
Links to Web sites about Roanoke, Jamestown, Williamsburg, Philadelphia, North Carolina; historical figures such as Anne Hutchinson and William Penn; documents (including maps); colonial trades, crafts, and lifestyles; religion; and resources for teachers.

Colonial Williamsburg: www.williamsburg.com/james/james.html
Historical background and information about visiting Colonial Williamsburg (a reconstructed colonial village in Virginia).

Colonization: edtech.kennesaw.edu/web/coloniz.html
Web Quests (Internet research projects), lesson plans, quizzes, and links.

Early America: www.earlyamerica.com
Primary documents, articles, and other information about 18th-century America.

Henry Ford Museum and Greenfield Village: www.hfmgv.org/smartfun/colonial/intro/index.html
Investigation, detective-style, of a real 18th-century Connecticut family.

History Online: www.jacksonesd.k12.or.us/k12projects/jimperry/colony.htm
Links to sites about Plymouth Colony, Jamestown, the Salem witch trials, Benjamin Franklin, and more.

Jamestowne Society: www.jamestowne.org
History of Jamestown written by descendants of settlers.

Kid Info: www.kidinfo.com/American_History/colonization_Jamestown.html
Extensive links on Virginia history, Jamestown Colony, colonial life, Native Americans in colonial times, slavery in colonial times, and more.

Powhatan History: www.powhatan.org/history
Includes Powhatan version of Pocahontas myth, historical background, and information about Powhatans today. For information on publications and festivals, contact: Powhatan Renape Nation, Rankokus Indian Reservation, P.O. Box 225, Rancocas, NJ 08703.

Virtual Jamestown: jefferson.village.virginia.edu/vcdh/jamestown
Primary documents (laws, census data, contracts, maps, art), historians' accounts of the settlement, a global time line, and resources (including teaching materials).

Courageous Colony Cards

Examination Card

In 1607, 105 males landed at Chesapeake Bay on the *Susan Constant*, the *Discovery* and what other ship?

a. *the Godspeed*
b. the Mayflower*
c. the Bounty**

*landed at Plymouth in 1620
**famous 18th-century ship

Examination Card

What company sponsored the Jamestown settlement?

a. the East India Company*
b. the Massachusetts Bay Company**
c. *the Virginia Company*

*trading company with a tea monopoly in the late 1700s
**Puritan sponsors

Examination Card

Why was the Jamestown colony founded?

a. *business (to make money)*
b. religious freedom*
c. prison colony**

*reason for Massachusetts colony
**reason for colonization of Australia

Examination Card

The Virginia Company paid their colonists a wage for being settlers, but it would <u>not</u> allow them to do what?

a. search for gold*
b. *own property*
c. harm Native Americans

*a main purpose of the settlement

Examination Card

Wahunsonacock was the ruler of five Algonquian groups in the Chesapeake Bay. What did the English colonists call him?

a. Metacom or Metacomet*
b. Samoset
c. *Powhatan*

*sachem of the Wampanoags

Examination Card

To stay out of sight of the Spanish Navy, English settlers chose an inland site along a river. What was the name of the river?

a. *James River*
b. Chesapeake River
c. Virginia River

Examination Card

The site of Jamestown was good for defense, but the swampy land was a huge drawback in what way?

a. It was not farmable.
b. *Mosquitoes transmitted malaria, a serious disease.*
c. It was not near a river.

Examination Card

What strict leader of Jamestown said, "If any would not work, neither should he eat."

a. John Rolfe*
b. *Captain John Smith*
c. Christopher Newport**

*husband of Pocahontas
**brought settlers to Virginia

Examination Card

What was the nickname given to the winter of 1609–1610?.

a. Thanksgiving, due to an abundance of food
b. *the Starving Time, due to a lack of food*
c. the Fighting Time, due to constant bickering between the colonists

---

Examination Card

After the Starving Time, colonists left Jamestown, and then met up with Lord De La Warr. What did he order them to do?

a. return to England
b. *return to the colony*
c. give up their Virginia Company wages

Examination Card

John Smith arranged the exchange of Tom Savage, an English boy, and Namontack, a Powhatan. What role did they play?

a. spies
b. couriers (messengers)
c. *interpreters (translators)*

Examination Card

After being kidnapped and held by Jamestown colonists, Pocahontas takes the name "Rebecca" to show her conversion to what religion?

a. *Christianity*
b. Judaism
c. Puritanism

Examination Card

In 1623, Captain William Tucker and his accomplice, Dr. John Potts, poisoned 200 Powhatans in a "toast" to what event?

a. the wedding of John Rolfe and Pocahontas
b. *a new peace treaty*
c. a successful tobacco crop

Examination Card

Because many people invested in the Virginia Company, what kind of company was it?

a. *joint stock company*
b. monopoly
c. cooperative company

Examination Card

In 1614, Jamestown shipped a crop to England for the first time and became economically successful. What was the crop?

a. cotton
b. indigo (a blue dye that comes from a plant)
c. *tobacco*

Examination Card

In 1619, the first boatload of women arrived at Jamestown. If a man married one of these women, who paid for this privilege?

a. The women paid.
b. *The men paid.**
c. No one paid.

*marriage cost 120 to 150 pounds of tobacco, the local currency

Courageous Colony Cards

Happenstance Card
Fire wipes out the thatch and wattle houses. Clothing goes up in flames during a frigid winter. Go back three spaces.

Happenstance Card
Mosquitoes transmit malaria to many colonists. The disease kills or weakens them. Go back three spaces.

Happenstance Card
Typhoid fever and dysentery run rampant. Only 38 of the original 105 colonists survive. Go back three spaces.

Happenstance Card
Most colonists are soldiers, gentry, servants, or artisans. Few know how to grow food. Go back three spaces.

Happenstance Card
Jamestown fort, shaped in a triangle, offers protection from attack. Go ahead two spaces and end your turn.

Happenstance Card
Colonists celebrate the first wedding between Anne Buras and John Laydon. Go ahead two spaces and end your turn.

Happenstance Card
A new leader, Thomas Gates, moves the colony to a healthier spot upriver. Go ahead two spaces and end your turn.

Happenstance Card
John Rolfe marries Matoaka, or Pocahontas. A brief time of peace follows. Go ahead two spaces and end your turn.

Examination Card
In 1619, a law-making body was set up as the first European representative government in the colonies. What was it called?

a. the Assembly*
b. *the House of Burgesses*
c. the House of Lords

*Massachusetts governing body

Examination Card
In 1624, King James closed down the joint stock Virginia Company. Investors lost their money. Jamestown officially becomes what type of colony?

a. proprietary
b. *royal*
c. independent

Examination Card
What explorer founded the failed colony of Roanoke years before Jamestown?

a. Captain James Cook*
b. Sir Frances Drake**
c. *Sir Walter Raleigh*

*18th-century explorer
**privateer and explorer who sailed around the world

Examination Card
A hurricane wrecked a ship called *Sea Venture* carrying new colonists. All survived. What admiral built two new ships out of the wreckage?

a. *Christopher Newport*
b. Christopher Columbus*
c. Christopher Robin

*15th-century explorer

Examination Card
Many people paid their way to the colonies by being indentured servants. What was an indentured servant?

a. slave
b. proprietor (owner)
c. *contract laborer*

*They worked 4 to 7 years to pay their passage, then were free.

Examination Card
A new variety of Virginia tobacco became popular in England. What Jamestown colonist developed the crop?

a. *John Rolfe*
b. Thomas Savage
c. Reverend Alexander Whitaker

Examination Card
On Good Friday, March 22, 1622, 350 Jamestown colonists died. How?

a. *attack by Powhatans*
b. typhoid epidemic
c. hurricane

*led by Opechancanough, Powhatan's brother and the uncle of Pocahontas

Examination Card
The charter of Virginia guaranteed English rights to any colonist born where?

a. in England only
b. *in the colonies, no matter the country of origin*
c. in the colonies, if the parents were English

Examination Card
Pocahontas was the nickname of Powhatan's daughter. What was her real name?

a. *Matoaka*
b. Opechancanough*
c. Sacagawea

*the name of her uncle, Powhatan's brother

Examination Card
Early colonists found food that was "very large and delicate in taste" and "as thick as stones." What food?

a. *oysters*
b. bears
c. truffles

*in addition to huge strawberries and wild grapevines

Examination Card
The Powhatan Confederacy was an alliance of peoples who shared a language and ethnic identity. What is this ethnic identity called?

a. Sioux or "little snake"
b. *Renape or "human beings"*
c. Iroquois or "real adders"

Examination Card
On March 22, 1622, a Powhatan boy named Chanco tried to save colonists' lives. How?

a. *by warning them of a surprise attack*
b. by showing them how to plant corn
c. by giving them medicine

*His warning did save some lives.

Hear Ye, Hear Ye!

☝ Revolutionary War News Game ☝

Players are news-hungry tavern-goers during the Revolutionary War. Their goal is to collect the facts of a major news story—who, what, where, when, and a quotation—by trading cards with other tavern-goers.

Materials

Players: 4 to 6 individuals or small groups (2 to 4 students per group), plus a game monitor

🛡 Hear Ye! Hear Ye! Cards (pages 42–46)

🛡 Hear Ye! Hear Ye! Answer Key and Optional Spinner (page 47)

🛡 (Optional) spinner, reference sources

Objectives

Historical Perspectives (Comprehending the Past) and Inquiry (Conducting Investigations): Identify and gather information about six Revolutionary War events. Place major events in chronological order.

Language Arts: Work cooperatively to orally state a news story based on facts. Write and research a news story (extension).

Preparation

Class or Large Group Play:

1. Divide students into four to six groups and ask each group to give itself a name and elect a messenger (someone to pass cards to other groups). Name suggestions: The Inn Syncs, Goose Gossip Inn, News World Inn, Never Diss Lodge, Tavern on the Stream, Tattler Tavern, Will-U-Whisper Tavern.

2. Photocopy and cut out the Hear Ye! Hear Ye! cards. **Note that you need to photocopy the last two pages of the set twice.** For six groups, use all 42 cards. For four or five groups, eliminate any two duplicate cards for a total of 40 cards.

3. Keep a copy of the answer key for your reference or give it to the game monitor.

Individual Play:

1. Make one set of cards per playing group. For six players, use all 42 cards. For four or five

players, eliminate any two duplicate cards for a total of 40 cards.

2. Conceal a copy of the answer key (page 47) in an envelope and give it to the dealer.

How to Play the Game

1. The dealer or game monitor shuffles the deck and deals out all cards evenly. Allow players time to read their cards, group any cards with a matching story line together, and decide which card to pass first. They might want to use references to look up or confirm facts.

2. To start each round of passing, the game monitor or dealer says, "Hear Ye! Hear Ye! Pass one card to the tavern on the right!" At the same time, each player or messenger passes one card to the player or group on the right. Players must pass a card, whether they are ready or not.

3. Players have about one minute to read their new card and decide which card to pass in the next round. After one minute is up, the game monitor or dealer again says, "Hear Ye! Hear Ye! Pass one card to the tavern on the right!"

4. Repeat step 3 until a player or group has a matching set of five cards (who, when, where, what, quotation) for one of the six stories and cries, "Hear ye! Hear ye! I (We) have news for all!" The game monitor or dealer makes sure all the cards pertain to the same story. (See the answer key, page 47.) If so, the player or group must tell the story, town-crier style, in order to win. (See the USHistory.org site under "Web Links.")

5. To complete their sets, the other players or groups can trade cards at will. Remind them that the winner has extra cards to trade.

Variations

Free Trade Version: A slightly more complicated but exciting version is to use a spinner (page 47) to randomly choose the number of cards and the direction for each round of passing.

Create a Colonial Atmosphere: Photocopy the game cards onto "antique-style" paper. Have groups design and create a sign for their tavern. As the game monitor announces each round of passing, he or she can ring a bell, as a town crier would. Winners can also use the bell to announce their news story.

Extensions

Newswriting: Whether or not students play the game, they can use a set of cards as a starting point to write a news story. Ask: Which of the five "W's" is missing from your set? (*why*) How can you find out the "why" for your story? Point out that each card has a "Look It Up" research question related to the information on the card. Have students work in groups to research the questions and gather other facts for their story.

Assemble the stories, chronologically, in a booklet. To make the booklet look authentic, use type faces and clip art similar to the design of newspaper documents of the day. Some of the Web sites listed on page 50 for the "Spy Versus Spy: Revolutionary War Research Game" include images to

print out or use for reference.

More Major News Events: Working in small groups, have students research and write a set of cards for another Revolutionary War news event. Tape their facts over the facts on the cards, making sure each fact matches the category at the top (who, what, where, when, quotation). Duplicate two of the cards. Then photocopy the set. Here are a few headlines to get students started:

- British Defeat Rebels at Bunker Hill (June 17, 1775)
- Paine's *Common Sense* an Instant Best-seller (January 9, 1776)
- Washington's Troops Fall at Battle of Brooklyn (August 27, 1776)
- Nathan Hale, Accused Spy, Is Hanged (September 22, 1776)
- "Stars and Stripes" Adopt U.S. Flag (June 14, 1777)
- British Surrender at Saratoga (October 17, 1777)
- France to Britain: It's War! (June 17, 1778)
- Washington Defeats Clinton at Monmouth Courthouse (June 28, 1778)
- Benedict Arnold, Patriot, Weds Peggy Shippen, Tory (April 9, 1779)
- Spain to Britain: It's War! (June 23, 1779)
- Treason! Arnold Betrays Patriots, Escapes Capture (September 21, 1780)
- Treaty of Paris Signed (September 3, 1783)

American Library Association: www.ala.org/parentspage/greatsites/
Click on "Great Sites" and then "People Past and Present" for recommended Web sites about history from pre-Columbian to 1865.

Revolutionary War: home.ptd.net/~revwar/index.html
Chronological list of battles, primary-source documents (including newspaper articles, journals, and public addresses), links, and other reference material.

USHistory.org: www.libertynet.org
Links to nonprofit sites related to 18th-century America and the Revolutionary War, a history bookstore, and more by a history organization based in Philadelphia. Click on "Town Criers" to hear audio clips from an annual town crier competition.

WHO? WHAT? WHERE? **WHEN?** QUOTATION

Early morning to dusk on
April 19, 1775

Look It Up: Francis Smith and 700 British soldiers began marching from what is now East Cambridge toward Concord at 2:00 a.m. Make a time line of events from that early morning march to dusk.

WHO? WHAT? WHERE? **WHEN?** QUOTATION

Just before dawn on
May 10, 1775

Look It Up: At what stage is the Revolutionary War on this date: beginning, middle, or end? What other important political event happened on this same day in Philadelphia, Pennsylvania?

WHO? WHAT? WHERE? **WHEN?** QUOTATION

July 4, 1776

Look It Up: On what date did delegates sign the Declaration of Independence? Why didn't the Continental Congress print and distribute the Declaration until January of the following year?

WHO? WHAT? WHERE? **WHEN?** QUOTATION

The bitter cold winter of
1777–78

Look It Up: What battles took place on September 11, 1777, and October 4, 1777? Who won? What is the average temperature and amount of snowfall for January in Philadelphia, Pennsylvania?

WHO? WHAT? WHERE? **WHEN?** QUOTATION

September 23, 1779

Look It Up: American warships sailed under the "Stars and Stripes," the flag of the Continental troops. How many stars and how many stripes did the flag have on this date?

WHO? WHAT? WHERE? **WHEN?** QUOTATION

At 12:00 noon on
October 19, 1781

Look It Up: What happened in Yorktown, Virginia, in the days preceding October 19? What happened in the days afterward?

WHO? **WHAT?** WHERE? WHEN? QUOTATION

At dawn, British troops defeat **Captain John Parker** and a colonial militia at Lexington. The British march to Concord, but are surrounded and forced to retreat to Lexington and, finally, to Boston by dusk. The American Revolution has begun!

Look It Up: What happened that afternoon at Hardy's Hill in an area known as Bloody Angle?

WHO? **WHAT?** WHERE? WHEN? QUOTATION

Before dawn, **Ethan Allen**, **Benedict Arnold**, and their men take Fort Ticonderoga from the British by surprise attack.

Look It Up: Who built the fort? How and when did the British gain control of it? What did the patriots gain from their victory?

WHO? **WHAT?** WHERE? WHEN? QUOTATION

The **Second Continental Congress** adopts the Declaration of Independence, a document outlining charges against George III of England and the principles of natural rights, including life, liberty, and property.

Look It Up: Who wrote the first draft of the Declaration? What other four men assisted?

WHO? **WHAT?** WHERE? WHEN? QUOTATION

Thousands of troops of the Continental Army, under the command of **General George Washington**, suffer without proper clothes or food through a bitter cold winter.

Look It Up: What advantages did the Continental Army have over the British Army? Who was Baron Friedrich von Steuben of Germany?

WHO? **WHAT?** WHERE? WHEN? QUOTATION

American warships, under command of **John Paul Jones**, attack a convoy of British ships. Though Jones' ship sinks under heavy attack, the British surrender in the first major victory of the American navy.

Look It Up: What is a broadside? What is a powder monkey? How did British powder monkeys on the *Serapis* unknowingly contribute to their own defeat?

WHO? **WHAT?** WHERE? WHEN? QUOTATION

Washington and the Continental Army, with help from French troops, trap British forces on a peninsula. After a long battle, the British surrender, ending the war.

Look It Up: What French military leaders aided Washington? Who was Nathanael Greene? Why didn't Sir Henry Clinton, commander of the British forces, help his trapped troops?

WHO? WHAT? WHERE? WHEN? **QUOTATION**

At Lexington, **Captain John Parker** is reported to have told the minutemen, "Don't fire unless fired upon. But if they want a war, let it begin here!"

Look It Up: What was "the shot heard 'round the world"? How did the fighting style of the minutemen differ from that of the British?

WHO? WHAT? WHERE? WHEN? **QUOTATION**

Jocelyn Feltham, a British lieutenant, has been asleep and is still in his underclothes. He asks on whose authority **Ethan Allen** is acting. Allen cries, "In the name of the Great Jehovah and the Continental Congress!"

Look It Up: What is the Second Continental Congress and when was it formed?

WHO? WHAT? WHERE? WHEN? **QUOTATION**

On June 7, 1776, **Richard Henry Lee**, a delegate from Virginia to the Continental Congress, offers forth this resolution: "That these United Colonies are, and of right ought to be, free and independent States."

Look It Up: Summarize in your own words the points made in the Declaration of Independence.

WHO? WHAT? WHERE? WHEN? **QUOTATION**

An **army surgeon** describes the scene: "There comes a soldier, his bare feet are seen through his worn-out stockings, his britches not sufficient to cover his nakedness."

Look It Up: How did other witnesses describe conditions at Valley Forge in diaries or letters?

WHO? WHAT? WHERE? WHEN? **QUOTATION**

Though the entire crew of the *Bonhomme Richard* knows the *Serapis* is a better warship, **John Paul Jones** refuses to surrender, saying, "I have not yet begun to fight!"

Look It Up: Describe the sea battle in your own words. Which ships sank? What major mistake did the American ship *Alliance* make?

WHO? WHAT? WHERE? WHEN? **QUOTATION**

Cornwallis writes to commander-in-chief Henry Clinton: "I have the mortification to inform your Excellency that I have been forced to . . . surrender the troops under my command, by capitulation . . . to the combined forces of America and France."

Look It Up: What do "mortification" and "capitulation" mean? Why do you think he chose those words?

WHO? WHAT? WHERE? WHEN? QUOTATION

Captain John Parker and a colonial militia (also known as minutemen), British officers **Francis Smith**, **John Pitcairn**, and their troops

Look It Up: What were the British officers' orders, given by their commander General Thomas Gage?

WHO? WHAT? WHERE? WHEN? QUOTATION

Major General and patriot **Ethan Allen**, his **Green Mountain Boys**, and **Colonel Benedict Arnold** of the Continental Army

Jocelyn Feltham, a British lieutenant

Look It Up: Who were the Green Mountain Boys and where did they come from? Find the Green Mountains on a map of the U.S.

WHO? WHAT? WHERE? WHEN? QUOTATION

The **Second Continental Congress**, a government set up to protect and advance American interests, including America's conflict with the British

Look It Up: How long did the First Continental Congress last? What major actions did the Second Continental Congress take during the war?

WHO? WHAT? WHERE? WHEN? QUOTATION

General George Washington, commander-in-chief, and his Continental Army

Look It Up: If you were Washington, how would you boost the morale of your troops? If you were a soldier at Valley Forge, how would you cope with the harsh conditions?

WHO? WHAT? WHERE? WHEN? QUOTATION

Captain John Paul Jones of the warship *Bonhomme Richard* ("Poor Richard")

Look It Up: Where did the name of the ship come from? Find three details about the life of John Paul Jones. What country was he born in? Why did he immigrate to America? What serious crime was he charged with early in life?

WHO? WHAT? WHERE? WHEN? QUOTATION

General George Washington, commander-in-chief, and his Continental Army

Look It Up: Whose side in the war did France take? What allies did Great Britain have? Who were Anthony Wayne, Horatio Gates, and Henry Knox?

WHO? WHAT? **WHERE?** WHEN? QUOTATION

Concord, **Lexington**, and **Boston, Massachusetts**, and areas in between

Look It Up: Find those cities on a map. How many miles is it between them? At about two miles per hour, how long would it take to walk from Concord to Boston?

WHO? WHAT? **WHERE?** WHEN? QUOTATION

Fort Ticonderoga on the southern tip of Lake Champlain in New York

Look It Up: What waterways are connected to Lake Champlain? To what country do these waterways lead? Why was the location of this fort important?

WHO? WHAT? **WHERE?** WHEN? QUOTATION

The Pennsylvania State House in Philadelphia, Pennsylvania, the American capital

Look It Up: The State House was renamed to reflect an important political event that took place there. What is its current name?

WHO? WHAT? **WHERE?** WHEN? QUOTATION

Valley Forge, Pennsylvania, a town about 24 miles northwest of Philadelphia, the American capital

Look It Up: Find Valley Forge on a map of the U.S. What type of terrain is it? Where did troops get drinking water?

WHO? WHAT? **WHERE?** WHEN? QUOTATION

The North Sea, off the northeastern coast of England near Flamborough Head and Scarborough

Look It Up: Find this location on a map. Why did American warships patrol these faraway waters?

WHO? WHAT? **WHERE?** WHEN? QUOTATION

Yorktown, which is on a peninsula in Chesapeake Bay, Virginia

Look It Up: How and why did more than 7,000 British troops end up in Yorktown? What route did Lord Cornwallis's army take to get there?

Hear Ye! Hear Ye! Answer Key and Optional Spinner

	WHO?	WHAT?	WHERE?	WHEN?	SPEAKER
1	Captain John Parker, the colonial militia, Frances Smith, John Pitcairn	The battles of Concord and Lexington	Concord; Lexington; and Boston, Massachusetts	April 19, 1775	Captain John Parker
2	Ethan Allen, the Green Mountain Boys, Benedict Arnold, Jocelyn Feltham	Attack on Fort Ticonderoga	Fort Ticonderoga, New York	May 10, 1775	Ethan Allen
3	The Second Continental Congress	Declaration of Independence adopted.	Pennsylvania State House in Philadelphia	July 4, 1776	Richard Henry Lee
4	General George Washington and the Continental Army	American troops suffer through a bitter winter.	Valley Forge, Pennsylvania	Winter of 1777–78	An army surgeon
5	John Paul Jones	Royal Navy defeated in battle at sea.	North Sea	September 23, 1779	John Paul Jones
6	General George Washington and the Continental Army	The British surrender.	Yorktown, Virginia	October 19, 1781	Lord Cornwallis

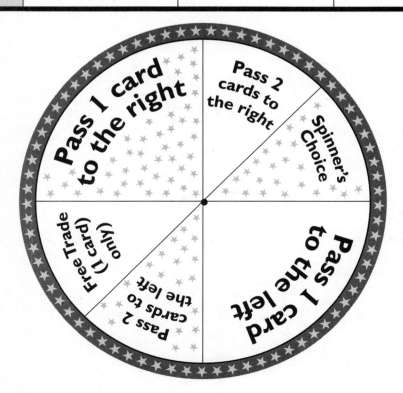

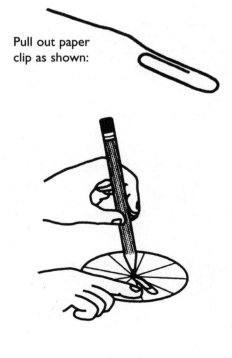

Pull out paper clip as shown:

Revolutionary War Research Game

Spy Versus Spy

☙ A Top Secret Internet and Book Search Challenge ❧

Teams of players are espionage agents who use their research skills to compile dossiers on enemy spies of the American Revolution. The more complete their dossiers, the higher their score.

Materials

Players: 2 or more groups, (3 to 6 students per group)

- ♜ Spy Versus Spy dossier form (page 51)
- ♜ Spy Versus Spy sample dossier form (page 52)
- ♜ reference sources including optional Internet access

Objectives

Historical Perspective (Comprehending the Past) and Inquiry (Conducting Investigations): Work cooperatively to research biographical information about figures in history.

Language Arts: Write a dossier (document with biographical facts), including primary source quotations.

Preparation

⚜ Make several copies per group of the Spy Versus Spy dossier form (page 51).

⚜ Gather other reference materials about people of the American Revolution. (See "Book Links.")

⚜ Search for and bookmark Web sites with biographical information about historic figures. (See "Web Links.")

⚜ Assign each group to either the Redcoat (British) or Patriot (American) side of the war and ask groups to create a code name. Suggestions: Spymasters, Rebel Web, Inner Net, Click and Dragger (in lieu of "cloak and dagger"), The Well-Read Coats.

⚜ Copy, distribute, and review the sample dossier on Jacques Cousteau (page 52), a World War II spy and famous ocean explorer.

How to Play the Game

⚜ Discuss resources that students can use to find out about Revolutionary spies, such as biographical books or Web sites, history books or Web sites, encyclopedias, primary source docu-

ments on the Web or in books, television documentaries, and historical magazines. Ask: What words should students look up in the indexes or tables of contents of a book? What words can they use for an Internet search? (*American Revolution*, *Revolutionary War*, *American history*, *spies*, *espionage*, *biographies*, and so on)

✡ Read and discuss the dossier form, emphasizing that teams are not expected to find all the information for every spy. Their goal is to find out as much as they can about as many enemy spies as they can. The more information they uncover, the more points they will score. (*Dossier*, pronounced doe-see-AY, is French for "bundle of detailed documents.")

✡ Refer, if necessary, to the following partial list of spies. (See "Web Links" and "Book Links.") Starred names are easier to research, since more information is available.

REDCOATS

*Major John André and other British intelligence officers
*Benedict Arnold
Ann Bates
Benjamin Church (double agent)
William Heron (Hiram the Spy)
Enoch Hoag
Francis Hogel
John Howe
Miss Jenny (code name of an unidentified French woman)

Simon Mabie
Nehemiah Marks
David Matthews (mayor of New York City)
*Major Pitcairn
William Showers
Daniel Taylor (silver bullet courier)
Benjamin Thompson (Count Rumford)
William Tryon (governor of New York)
Patrick Walker
Samuel Wallis

PATRIOTS

Ann Trotter Bailey
Elias Boudinot (Commissioner General of Prisoners)
Alexander Bryan
Lewis Costigin
Lydia Darragh and her 14-year-old son John (button courier)
Joshua Davis
*Sarah Bradlee Fulton ("the mother of the Boston Tea Party")
Emily Geiger
*Nathan Hale
*Alexander Hamilton
John Honeyman
*John Jay and others in the spy-catchers' ring
Isaac Ketcham

Thomas Knowlton (of Knowlton's Raiders)
Gen. Charles Lee
Hercules Mulligan
Number 355 (code name for a spy who was later revealed to be the wife of Robert Townsend, a Culper member)
Jonathan Odell
*John Parker
Joseph Reed
*Paul Revere and the Mechanics
Haym Salomon
*Joseph Stansbury
*Brig. Gen. Charles Scott and other American intelligence officers
*Major Benjamin Tallmadge and the Culper Gang

Collect and score the dossiers.

Variation

Easier, Shorter Version: Cut off the bottom half of the dossier form (questions 7 through 10) and have students fill in the top half only. Encourage students to conduct specific Internet searches using the names of the spies listed on page 49.

Extensions

Dossier Books: Compile the dossiers into two books, one for Patriot spies and one for Redcoat spies. Have students choose a spy and write a short historical-fiction story about his or her life.

Other Wars, Other Spies: The Spy Versus Spy dossier form is generic enough to use for investigating spies in other wars. For information on playing Spy Versus Spy: Civil War, see page 71.

American Women in Uniform: userpages.aug.com/captbarb/spies.html
Personal Web page with biographical information about military women from colonial times to the Space Age.

CIA Kids Page: www.odci.gov/cia/ciakids/history
Kids can decode secret messages, create disguises, research biographical information about spies, and more.

Discovery Channel:
school.discovery.com/fall98/activities/keyplayersoftherevolution/
Background and lesson plans.

History/Social Studies for K–12 Teachers:
www.execpc.com/~dboals/boals.html
Extensive links by topic, including a lengthy section of kids' sites.

Spies of the American Revolution: www.si.umich.edu/spies/index.html
Primary source documents, images, and short biographies of Revolutionary War spies.

BOOK LINKS

Black Heroes of the American Revolution by Burke Davis (Harcourt Brace, 1992). Profiles of spies, soldiers, scouts, guides, and others, for ages 9 to 12.

Finishing Becca: A Story About Peggy Shippen and Benedict Arnold ("American Colonies Series") by Ann Rinaldi (Gulliver, 1994). Historical fiction for young adults.

Spies of the Revolution by Katherine and John Bakeless (Scholastic, 1962). Out of print, but check your library for this excellent nonfiction title for young adults. A more challenging, adult resource is *Turncoats, Traitors, and Heroes* by J. Bakeless (Da Capo Press, 1998).

Those Remarkable Women of the American Revolution by Karen Zeinert (Millbrook, 1996). Profiles of soldiers, spies, heroes, and others, for young adults.

Top Secret Dossier by _____

(team's code name)

Spy Versus Spy

It's wartime! Enemy spies are everywhere: in biography books, history books, encyclopedias, historical magazines, and even on the Internet. You and your intelligence team can score up to 15 points for each enemy spy you find and document, using the dossier form below.

Meanwhile, your enemies will be looking for your spies. The team with the most points wins Spy Versus Spy!

1 Name of spy: _____ 2 Male or female ? (circle one)

3 Nationality :_____

4 Which side of the conflict was the spy loyal to? _____

5 Is a photo or drawing available? If so, tape or glue a copy on the back of this dossier.
  If you cannot copy the picture, trace it or make a drawing.

6 Describe the spy's appearance to help your troops identify him or her.
  (hair and eye color, clothing, height, weight, and the like)

7 How did the spy gather information about the enemy?
  (disguises, secret codes, undercover work, and the like)

8 Was the spy ever caught? Yes or no? (circle one) Provide details.

9 Quotation or written statement made by the spy or about the spy.

10 Details of the spy's life. (accomplishments, meetings with famous people, heroic acts, life before the war, family members, manner of death, and the like)

SCORE: _____ (For items 1-9, score 1 point each. Score up to 5 ponts for item 10.)   (Continue on the back, if needed.)

Spy Versus Spy

It's wartime! Enemy spies are everywhere: in biography books, history books, encyclopedias, historical magazines, and even on the Internet. You and your intelligence team can score up to 15 points for each enemy spy you find and document, using the dossier form below.

Meanwhile, your enemies will be looking for your spies. The team with the most points wins Spy Versus Spy!

1 Name of spy: _____ *Jacques-Yves Cousteau* _____ **2** (**Male**) **or female ? (circle one)**

3 Nationality : _____ *French* _____

4 Which side of the conflict was the spy loyal to? _____ *Allies* _____

5 Is a photo or drawing available? If so, tape or glue a copy on the back of this dossier. If you cannot copy the picture, trace it or make a drawing.

6 Describe the spy's appearance to help your troops identify him or her.
(hair and eye color, clothing, height, weight, and the like)

Cousteau was tall and thin with an exceedingly large nose, bright blue eyes, and a warm smile. He sometimes wore wire-rim glasses and, later in life, a multi-color set of pens in a pocket in his left shirtsleeve. As leader of the world's first SCUBA diving team, he often wore black wetsuits. His left arm was permanently damaged in a car accident.

7 How did the spy gather information about the enemy?
(disguises, secret codes, undercover work, and the like)

After Italy took control of southern France, Cousteau dressed in disguise as an Italian officer and snuck into an enemy base. He spent four hours photographing top-secret material while an accomplice distracted the Italian commander. Cousteau also used his diving abilities to gather intelligence on and sabotage enemy ships.

8 Was the spy ever caught? Yes or (**no?**) **(circle one) Provide details.**

Had an Italian guard talked to Cousteau, he would have quickly discovered that the French spy spoke little Italian. Capture would have meant the death penalty.

9 Quotation or written statement made by the spy or about the spy.

"Il faut aller voir." (We have to see for ourselves.) —Jacques Cousteau to his fellow divers

10 Details of the spy's life. (accomplishments, meetings with famous people, heroic acts, life before the war, family members, manner of death, and the like)

Cousteau's brother, Philippe, was a Nazi collaborator in World War II. The Allies imprisoned him for treason and condemned him to death, but released him years later after Philippe fell ill. Cousteau went on to fame and fortune as the captain of the Calypso, a research vessel that explored the world's oceans. He wrote dozens of books and made dozens of films and TV specials about sea life. He died in 1997, at age 87. His wife, Francine Cousteau, and his elder son, Jean-Michel, continue Cousteau's mission to preserve the oceans. His younger son, Philippe, died in an accident.

SCORE: _____ (For items 1-9, score 1 point each. Score up to 5 ponts for item 10.)   (Continue on the back, if needed.)

Law of the Land Scavenger Hunt

☙ A U.S. Constitution Race Game ☙

Teams race to locate specific information in the U.S. Constitution. Clues are provided on two levels of difficulty.

Materials

- ♛ Scavenger Hunt Cards (pages 55 and 56)
- ♛ 18 to 36 index cards (or similar-sized pieces of paper)
- ♛ tape
- ♛ U.S. Constitution (at least one copy per team)
- ♛ dictionary (one per team)
- ♛ (Optional) colored pens

Objectives

Civic Perspective (Purposes of Government; Ideals of American Democracy): Identify and reference the three branches of government as described in the Constitution. Identify the role of government, including provisions that delegate powers and provide for checks and balances.

Language Arts: Read and interpret the Constitution. Use reference sources to answer questions.

Preparation

1. Decide whether your students will play on the easier or harder level.

2. For the easier level (first three articles only, clues 1 through 18), photocopy and cut out the "easier" cards. For the harder level (all seven articles, clues 19 through 36), copy both sets of cards on different-colored paper and cut them out.

3. Tape or glue each question to the top of an index card. Shuffle or scramble the cards.

4. Divide students into small groups and ask each group to elect one messenger (to post answers, draw new cards, and look for errors or omissions on other teams' cards), one or two Researchers

(to look up answers), and a Writer/Researcher (to neatly record answers on the cards).

5 Ask each messenger to write a team name on the blackboard, leaving a space underneath to post cards. Suggestions: The Fast Federals, We the People, Freedom Forever, Liberty Belles, Righteous Racers, First Amendments, Justice Ringers. To make scoring easier, give each team a different-colored pen or marker.

6 Set a roll of clear tape near the board.

How to Play the Game

1 The game monitor randomly passes out one card per team. If you're playing on the harder level, teams can choose whether to receive an easier or harder card. Harder cards (clues 19 through 36) are worth double the points.

2 Teams search for the answer to their question in the Constitution and write it on the index card. They can use references to answer bonus questions. If teams get stuck, they can trade in their card for a new one.

3 Messengers tape the answered card on the board, under their team name, and draw a new card to take back to their team.

4 Teams play until all the cards are posted or until time runs out.

5 During game play, messengers can search other teams' answers for mistakes. If they find one, they write the answer on the card, along with their team's name.

6 After the last card is posted, the game monitor uses the master copy of pages 55 and 56 to check and review the answers with the class. He or she awards 1 point per correct answer and 2 points per correct bonus for easier cards, and doubles the points for harder cards. Incorrect answers score no points. If a team successfully challenges another team's answer, the challenging team scores double the point value of the answer.

Variations

Extra Challenge: Require the winners to recite the Preamble from memory in order to win the game. If they can't, the next higher scorer gets a chance to recite the text and win.

Easier Version: Photocopy the Constitution and highlight the sections addressed on the Easier Cards (page 55).

FindLaw Constitutional Law Center: supreme.findlaw.com
The U. S. Constitution, historic documents, Supreme Court cases, and more—all searchable.

The Internet Public Library's Presidents of the United States (reference): www.ipl.org/ref/POTUS

USA History: www.usahistory.com
Information about the Constitution, presidents, and more.

Law of the Land Scavenger Hunt (Easier Cards)

★

Item to find	Answer	Item to find	Answer
1. You are elected president in the year 2030. How many years will you serve? *Bonus:* In what month and year will the next president be sworn in?	Article II 1.1 4 years; January 2035	**10.** Suppose North and South Dakota go to court to decide which state is prettier. What high court will hear the case? *Bonus:* Where is the court located?	Article III 2.1 Supreme Court; Washington, D.C.
2. As president, you earn $200,000 per year. How much of a raise can you get while you're in office? *Bonus:* If you resign, who takes your place?	Article II 1.7 none; vice president	**11.** As president, you agree to "preserve, _____, and _____ the Constitution." *Bonus:* Who administers this oath of office to the president?	Article II 1.8 protect and defend; chief justice (of the Supreme Court)
3. You plan to run for the Senate as soon as you're old enough. How old do you have to be? *Bonus:* How old must Representatives be?	Article I 3.3 30; 25	**12.** Vera Young is 38 years old. Is she old enough to be president of the United States? *Bonus:* What is the minimum age for a president?	Article II 1.5 yes; 35
4. Terry Traitor is convicted of treason. Who will decide her punishment? *Bonus:* A president can be ousted from office for treason, bribery, and _____.	Article III 3.2 Congress; high crimes and misdemeanors	**13.** What is the collective name for the Senate and the House of Representatives? *Bonus:* Which group has more members?	Article I 1.0 Congress; House
5. As president, you're Chief Executive. Your military title is _____ of the Armed Forces. *Bonus:* Who was Chief Executive the year you were born?	Article II 2.1 Commander in Chief; Reagan 81–88; Bush 89–92; Clinton 93–00	**14.** You are head of the House of Representatives. What's your title? *Bonus:* If the president and vice president die, who takes over?	Article I 2.5 Speaker of the House; Speaker of the House
6. What is the name of the highest court in the U.S.? *Bonus:* How long can judges of that court hold their office?	Article III 1.1 Supreme Court; for life (or "during good behavior")	**15.** How many senators does your state have? *Bonus:* Name one of your current senators.	Article I 3.1 2; answers vary
7. Terry Traitor levied war against the United States. What's the name for Terry's crime? *Bonus:* What is bribery?	Article III 3.1 treason; illegal payment to corrupt an official	**16.** You are president of the Senate. What is your other title? *Bonus:* When is the only time you can vote in the Senate?	Article I 3.4 vice president of the U.S.; to break a tie
8. Terry Traitor adhered to enemies and gave them aid and comfort. What crime did Terry commit? *Bonus:* What does *adhere* mean?	Article III 3.1 treason; stick to, follow, be devoted to	**17.** Which branch of government has the power to coin money? *Bonus:* What is the official currency of the United States?	Article I 8.5 legislative (Congress); dollar (or U.S. dollar)
9. Ima Immigrant was born in Italy. Can she be president of the U.S.? *Bonus:* What is a naturalized citizen?	Article II 1.5 no; immigrant who becomes a citizen	**18.** Who has the power to make laws? *Bonus:* Who has the power to veto bills so that they do not become laws?	Article I 8.18 Congress; president

Law of the Land Scavenger Hunt (Harder Cards) ★

Item to find	Answer	Item to find	Answer
19. Who has both the power to lay (set) and collect income taxes and the duty to pay debts owed by the U.S.? *Bonus:* What is a deficit?	Article I 8.1 Congress; the amount of money short of what is needed	**28.** Who must inform Congress of the state of the union, usually in a televised address? *Bonus:* What is a rebuttal?	Article II 3.1 president, argument in opposition (in a debate, for example)
20. If you, as president, veto a bill, what fraction of each House must vote "yea" to make the bill a law? *Bonus:* What is a line-item veto?	Article I 7.2 two-thirds; veto of select parts of a bill	**29.** What special type of trial may not be held by jury? *Bonus:* What president was convicted in this type of trial in the 1990s?	Article III 2.3 impeachment; Clinton
21. Chris Criminal commits a federal crime in Utah. Will be he tried in Utah or in a federal court? *Bonus:* What is a felony?	Article III 2.3 Utah; crime punished by more than one year in prison	**30.** Vera Young is 38 years old. Is she old enough to be president? *Bonus:* The oldest president was first elected in 1980 at age 69. Who was he?	Article II 1.5 yes (35 years or older); Reagan
22. Terry Traitor didn't confess to treason. How many witnesses are needed to convict her of it? *Bonus:* Where must a treason confession take place?	Article III 3.1 two; open court	**31.** If the legislatures of Iowa and Idaho vote to unite into one state, who must approve the move? *Bonus:* What was the 50th state added to the Union?	Article IV 3.1 Congress; Hawaii
23. "We the people of the United States, in order to form a _____ . . ." *Bonus:* What year did the Constitution go into effect?	Preamble more perfect Union; 1789 (after ratification by nine states)	**32.** Chris Criminal commits murder in Michigan, but is caught in Ohio. Which state has the right to try the case? *Bonus:* What does *extradition* mean?	Article IV 2.2 Michigan; transfer of a prisoner from one state to another
24. What titles of nobility can Congress bestow on exceptional citizens? *Bonus:* What is a monarchy?	Article I 9.8 none; rule by a hereditary sovereign (king, queen, emperor, etc.)	**33.** To add an amendment to the Constitution, what fraction of states must approve it? *Bonus:* What is the minimum number of states (out of 50)?	Article V 1.1 three-fourths; 38
25. The president has "the power to grant _____ for offences against the U.S." *Bonus:* In 1974, Gerald Ford exercised this power for what former president?	Article II 2.1 reprieves and pardons; Nixon	**34.** "This constitution shall be . . . the supreme law of _____." *Bonus:* What is a treaty?	Article VI 2.0 the land; formal international agreement
26. What branch of government can declare war, punish pirates, and raise an army and navy? *Bonus:* Who establishes post offices?	Article I 8.10-13 legislative (Congress); Congress	**35.** Which legislative body has the sole power to try all impeachments? *Bonus:* What fraction of members must agree in order to convict an official?	Article I 3.6 Senate; two-thirds
27. Ima Immigrant has been a U.S. citizen for ten years. Can she run for president? *Bonus:* What is a Green Card?	Article II 1.4 no; ID for alien residents who are not citizens	**36.** In what year was the Constitution signed? *Bonus:* Within one year, how many years before that date did the American Revolution end?	Article VII 1.2 1787; four years (1783)

CHAPTER 3

West Quest 1, 2, and 3

🦅 3 Time-Line Puzzles About Westward Expansion 🦅

Players place fact cards in chronological order by reading clues about 19th century people and events. If placed correctly, the backs of the cards form a U.S. map of western expansion.

Materials

Players: individuals, partners, or small cooperative groups

🛡 West Quest cards (pages 59–61), U.S. map (page 62)

🛡 (Optional) reference sources, nonpermanent marker

Objectives

Historical Perspective (Time and Chronology): Place major events in the settlement of the West in chronological order. Identify cause-and-effect relationships.

Preparation

1. Photocopy each West Quest card deck (pages 59–61) onto a different-colored paper.

2. Photocopy the U.S. map (page 62) onto the backs of each card set. (This map provides the answer key at the end of the game: If the events are sequenced correctly, the map pieces will match when the cards are turned over.)

3. Cut out and laminate the cards.

4. Give one deck to each player, pair, or group of players.

How to Solve the Puzzles

1. All cards should be event-side up, map-side down, and shuffled.

2. If playing in groups, members should read each card aloud.

3. Using references, prior knowledge, and the clues on the cards, players arrange the cards in chronological order. Some students will discover that the card with "Clue to first card" is the

last card in the set. You might give them the answer to the first card to help them get started.

⚡ After students have all the cards in order, they should arrange them in two equal horizontal rows. (Decks 1 and 3: 2 rows of 5 cards; Deck 2: 2 rows of 6 cards.)

⚡ Players turn over each card in its place. If the order is correct, the cards will form a map of the U.S. Here are the dates of the events on the cards.

West Quest 1: Central United States

1803: Louisiana Purchase
1804–06: Corps of Discovery
1810–12: War Hawks
1819: "Great American Desert"
1825: Erie Canal Opens

1830: Indian Removal Act
1862: Homestead Act
1871: Americanization of Indians
1876: Custer's Defeat
1890: Wounded Knee Massacre

West Quest 2: Northwest, Hawaii, and Alaska

1811: Fort Astoria in Oregon Territory
1817–18: U.S.-Canada Border
1823: The Monroe Doctrine
1841: The Oregon Trail
1845: Manifest Destiny
1859: Oregon Statehood

1867: Alaska Purchase
1869: Transcontinental Railroad
1877: Chief Joseph Surrenders
1887: The Dawes Act
1898: Klondike Gold Rush
1959: Alaska and Hawaii Statehood

West Quest 3: Southwest and California

1822: The Santa Fe Trail
1825: Mexican Texas
1836: Texas Independence
1846–47: Mexican War
1848–49: California Gold Rush

1853: Gadsden Purchase
1886: Geronimo's Surrender
1890: Frontier Closes
1898: Spanish-American War
1912: Arizona and New Mexico Statehood

Variations

Easier Version: Have students assemble the map puzzle first. Then they can turn over the cards to see the finished time line. After studying the time line for a minute or two, challenge students to scramble the cards and put them back in the right order.

More Challenging Version: Have students research and record all the event names and dates on a separate sheet of paper for each set of cards. Encourage students to use this list to design an illustrated time line with one, two, or all of the sets of cards.

The American West: www.americanwest.com
Information about cowboys, Native Americans, pioneers, explorers, western art, and ghost towns.

Chinese-American History: www.itp.berkeley.edu/~asam121/timeline.html
Time line of events from 1848 to present.

Native American Sites: www.pitt.edu/~lmitten/indians.html
Link to the Web sites of many Native American nations.

PBS's *Lewis and Clark*: www.pbs.org/lewisandclark/

West Quest Cards

Louisiana Purchase

French emperor Napoleon sells the Louisiana Territory to the U.S., doubling the nation's size. President Thomas Jefferson is reelected the following year. He plans to map and explore the new land.

Clue to Next Card: Sacagawea, Shoshone guide and translator

Lewis and Clark's Corps of Discovery

Lewis and Clark lead an expedition through the Louisiana Territory to the Pacific Ocean. They meet Mandans, Shoshones, and many other peoples; make maps; and collect samples of plants and animals.

Clue to Next Card: Henry Clay, John Calhoun, Felix Grundy, and other congressmen

War Hawks

"War Hawk" congressmen pressure President James Madison to go to war with Britain. He does. The War of 1812 breaks out.

Clue to Next Card: Pike's Peak, Nebraska, and other Plains territories

The "Great American Desert" of the Plains

Stephen Long explores the Platte River and the dry, flat, treeless plains. He and explorer Zebulon Pike spread the belief that the Great Plains are not fit for settlement.

Clue to Next Card: The Hudson River to the Great Lakes

Erie Canal Opens

Begun in 1817, the canal links New York City to Buffalo on Lake Erie, allowing Midwest farm products to be sold more easily in the East.

Clue to Next Card: Black Hawk's War, Trail of Tears, Reservations

Indian Removal Act

Chippewa, Iowa, Sioux, Sac, Fox, and many other peoples are forced to give their lands to white settlers and move west into reservations. The last to leave the Southeast are the Cherokee, many of whom die on the long, hard journey.

Clue to Next Card: Sodbusters

Homestead Act

The U.S. government awards a 160-acre lot to anyone who farms the land for five years. The act results in fast settlement by farmers of the Great Plains, which is no longer known as "The Great American Desert."

Clue to Next Card: Carlisle Indian School, cultural deprivation

Americanization of Indians

The U.S. begins to treat Indians, or Native Americans, as "wards" of the government, forbidding them to speak their languages or follow traditional customs. Sarah Winnemucca and other reformers later protest this treatment.

Clue to Next Card: Little Bighorn, Montana

Custer's Defeat

The U.S. breaks its treaty with Sioux, Cheyenne, and Arapaho peoples, allowing white gold miners and settlers to move into Indian territory in the Black Hills. Warriors led by Sitting Bull and Crazy Horse kill 264 soldiers, including George Custer.

Clue to Next Card: Sioux ghost dancers

Wounded Knee Massacre

Fearing an uprising by a group of religious Sioux, U.S. troops slaughter men, women, and children at Wounded Knee Creek in South Dakota. The massacre was the last major conflict between the U.S. and Native Americans.

Clue to First Card: Mississippi River basin

West Quest Cards

Fort Astoria in Oregon Territory

John Jacob Astor, a wealthy New York fur merchant, builds Fort Astoria, the first American settlement in Oregon Territory. British Canada also wants to own and settle the territory.

Clue to Next Card: The 49th Parallel or Latitude, a dividing line and boundary

---

Alaska Purchase

The U.S. buys Alaska from Russia for the bargain price of $7.2 million. Most Americans think the frozen land is no bargain.

Clue to Next Card: Promontory, Utah, May 10, 1869

U.S.–Canada Border

After The War of 1812, the U.S. and British Canada agree on a border from Minnesota to the Rockies; however, Oregon Territory is left undecided. Both American and British families settle there.

Clue to Next Card: Nationalism (pro-American sentiment)

Transcontinental Railroad

The final gold and silver spikes are driven into the first coast-to-coast railroad in the U.S. at Promontory Point, Utah.

Clue to Next Card: "From where the sun now stands, [I] will fight no more forever."

The Monroe Doctrine

To keep America's borders safe, President James Monroe warns Russia not to expand its Alaska holdings down the Pacific Coast.

Clue to Next Card: Conestoga wagon, Independence Rock

Chief Joseph Surrenders

The U.S. government forces the Nez Percé off their eastern Oregon lands, triggering a revolt led by Chief Joseph. Hundreds try to escape to Canada, but after enduring months of extreme hardship, they surrender.

Clue to Next Card: Failed Reform

The Oregon Trail

Pioneers traveled from Independence, Missouri, along the Platte River, across the Rocky Mountains, along the Snake and Columbia Rivers, and to the Oregon Territory.

Clue to Next Card: Expansionists

The Dawes Act

The U.S. government divides Indian reservations into individually owned farm plots. This effort to aid Indians backfires when most of the land is sold to white settlers.

Clue to Next Card: Joseph Juneau, prospector and miner

Manifest Destiny

A magazine writer uses the term "manifest destiny" to describe a future U.S. that spans from coast to coast. U.S. citizens support the idea of expanding their nation.

Clue to Next Card: In 1859, the Beaver State joins the Union.

Klondike Gold Rush

The discovery of gold inspires some 30,000 people to move to Alaska, which is owned by the U.S. Alaska becomes a U.S. territory 15 years later.

Clue to Next Card: The Last Frontier and the Aloha State join the Union.

Oregon Statehood

Thirteen years after the U.S.–Canadian border is partly drawn, Oregon becomes a state. Neighboring Washington would not do so for another 30 years.

Clue to Next Card: Seward's Folly or Seward's Icebox at two cents per acre

---

Alaska, Hawaii Are States

Alaska and Hawaii become the 49th and 50th states. Puerto Rico, Guam, and the U.S. Virgin Islands, remain territories.

Clue to First Card: Beaver trapping and fur trading make trappers millionaires.

West Quest Cards

WEST QUEST 3

The Santa Fe Trail

William Becknell leads a caravan from Missouri to Santa Fe, New Mexico, forging a new trail across desert wilderness for traders and settlers.

Clue to Next Card: Stephen Austin, impresario, brings settlers to Texas, owned by Mexico.

WEST QUEST 3

Gadsden Purchase

The U.S. buys part of Arizona and New Mexico from Mexico and builds train tracks to California's Pacific coast.

Clue to Next Card: To the Pueblos, the name *apachu* means "the enemy."

WEST QUEST 3

Mexican-Owned Texas

Mexico allows American settlers to move into Texas, provided they are loyal to Mexico and practice the Catholic religion. The settlers are mostly slave owners from the South who grow cotton and other crops.

Clue to Next Card: Battle of the Alamo, the Lone Star Republic

WEST QUEST 3

Geronimo Surrenders

Geronimo and his Apache warriors surrender, after a long war to hold on to their land in what is now the American Southwest. After their surrender the U.S. government moved Geronimo and his people to the White Mountain Reservation in Arizona.

Clue to Next Card: The 98th degree of longitude splits the U.S. into the East and the settled West.

WEST QUEST 3

Texas Independence

Texans declare independence from Mexico and form a republic. Sam Houston leads the Texan army in defeating Santa Anna of Mexico. Texans govern themselves.

Clue to Next Card: Zachary Taylor, "Old Rough and Ready," heads the U.S. Army.

WEST QUEST 3

The Frontier Closes

The U.S. Census Bureau announces that the frontier is closed, since homesteaders have settled most of the West.

Clue to Next Card: "Remember the Maine!" and Teddy Roosevelt's Rough Riders

WEST QUEST 3

Mexican War

The republic of Texas joins the U.S. as a state, leading to war with Mexico in 1846. Californians also revolt and declare themselves "The Bear Flag Republic."

Clue to Next Card: Forty-niners, Sutter's mill

WEST QUEST 3

Spanish-American War

In support of Cuban and Puerto Rican revolts against Spanish rule, the U.S. declares war on Spain. As a result, the U.S. gains Puerto Rico, Guam, and the Philippines. Cuba later becomes independent.

Clue to Next Card: The Land of Enchantment and the Grand Canyon State join the Union.

WEST QUEST 3

California Gold Rush

The discovery of gold causes floods of people to move to California. The U.S. buys California, Nevada, Utah, Texas, and parts of Colorado, Wyoming, Arizona, and New Mexico from Mexico, which lost the Mexican War.

Clue to Next Card: Southwest train route through newly bought land

WEST QUEST 3

New Mexico, Arizona are States

New Mexico and Arizona become U.S. states. Both areas were first explored and settled in the 1520s and settled in the early 1600s by Spain.

Clue to First Card: Desert trailblazer

West Quest Map: U.S. Westward Expansion ★

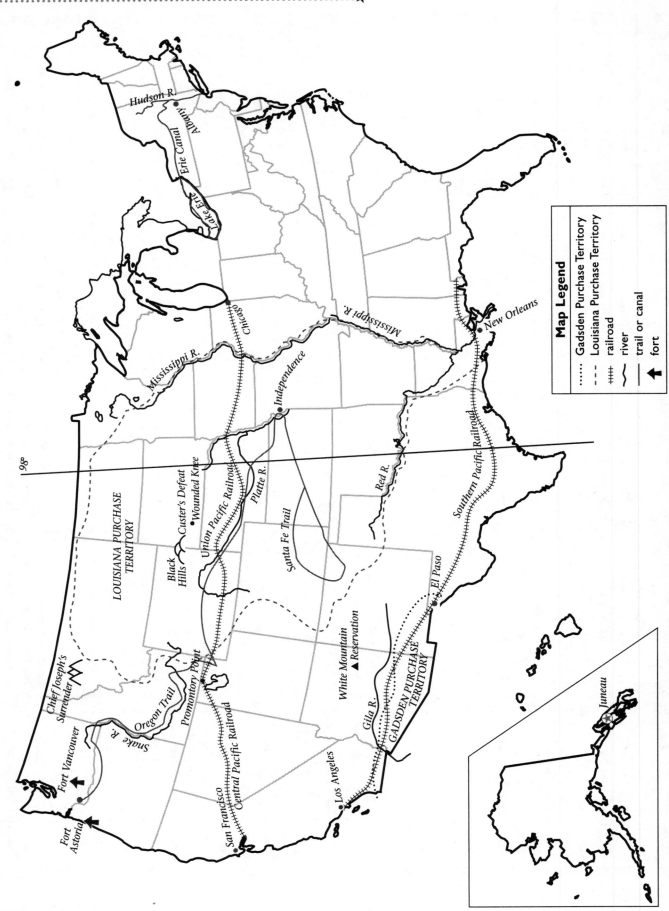

Map Legend

- ⋯⋯⋯ Gadsden Purchase Territory
- – – – Louisiana Purchase Territory
- +++ railroad
- ⌒ river
- —— trail or canal
- ← fort

Hudson R.

Albany

Erie Canal

Lake Erie

Chicago

Mississippi R.

Mississippi R.

New Orleans

Independence

98°

LOUISIANA PURCHASE TERRITORY

Custer's Defeat
Wounded Knee

Union Pacific Railroad

Platte R.

Black Hills

Santa Fe Trail

Red R.

Southern Pacific Railroad

El Paso

White Mountain ▲ Reservation

Chief Joseph's Surrender

Oregon Trail

Promontory Point

Snake R.

Fort Vancouver

San Francisco

Central Pacific Railroad

Los Angeles

Gila R.

GADSDEN PURCHASE TERRITORY

Fort Astoria

Juneau

North or South?

❧ A Civil War Fact Classification Game ❧

Players take turns deciding whether facts (e.g., "cannonballs bounced harmlessly off ironclad ships") apply to the North, the South, or both sides in the Civil War. The player with the most correct answers wins.

Materials

🛡 North or South Fact Cards/Battle of the Brains Question Cards (pages 67–70), including three TEAM cards

🛡 (Optional) two hula hoops

Objectives

Historical Perspective (Comprehending the Past): Use prior knowledge to identify and classify events and people. Recall and understand information about the Civil war.

Math: Make a Venn diagram by classifying facts into three groups.

Preparation

1️⃣ Photocopy the side 1A and 1B cards (pages 67 and 68) back to back onto card stock or stiff paper. Photocopy the side 2A and 2B cards (pages 69 and 70) back to back on the same type of paper. *Note that correctly aligning double-sided copies may be difficult.* One alternative is to make permanent cards from the pages of this book (be sure to keep additional copies of these pages on hand!): simply laminate the aligned back-to-back pages (67/68 and 69/70), cut out the cards, and store them for future use in an envelope. Another option is to photocopy each page, correctly align the paired pages back to back, and glue them together.

2️⃣ Cut out all the cards on the solid lines and fold them in half on the dotted lines to form tents. The FACT sides should be facing out; the questions should be on the inside.

3️⃣ Place the three TEAM cards in a row in the center of the playing space so that the "Team 1" sides face Team 1 and "Team 2" sides face Team 2. Stack the rest of the cards in random order in a single pile.

How to Play the Game

⭐ One player (or team) draws the top card of the FACT stack and reads the fact aloud. The other player (or team) must decide if the fact applies to the North, the South, or both sides and place the card next to his or her corresponding TEAM card.

⭐ Players take turns drawing, reading, and placing cards in this manner until all the stack has been exhausted.

⭐ Players score 1 point for each correct answer. The answers are on the insides of the cards, at the top. If an answer is "Both," it does not belong with either "North" or "South"; it belongs next to the card marked "Both." (Tell students to disregard the Infantry, Cavalry, and Officer points for now; those come into place for the Battle of the Brains game.)

⭐ The team or player with the greatest number of correct answers wins.

Variation

Venn Version: To emphasize classification, use two hula hoops (or circles of yarn) to form a Venn diagram around the three TEAM cards in the center. One hoop circles the North card, the other hoop circles the South card, and the two hoops overlap in the center to form a space for the 'Both' card.

Extension

Battle of the Brains: The Battle of the Brains game (next page) is an excellent follow-up to this game, since the questions build on the facts students have just learned. If students play both games in a row, they can combine their scores to determine an overall winner.

History Place: www.historyplace.com/civilwar/
Civil War time line and other background.

U.S. Civil War Center: www.cwc.lsu.edu/cwc/civlink.htm
The site lists more than 4,500 links to Civil War Web sites. The above address takes you directly to the biographical links.

Battle of the Brains

☙ A Civil War Question–and–Answer Strategy Game ☙

Players win each other's cards by answering questions correctly on three levels of difficulty. Hidden cards (bomb, spy, and president) add strategy and suspense.

Materials

Players: 2 individuals or 2 pairs of students

♛ North or South Fact Cards/Battle of the Brains Question Cards (pages 67–70), including three TEAM cards

Objective

Historical Perspective (Comprehending the Past): Use prior knowledge to identify and classify events and people. Recall and understand information about the Civil War.

Preparation

❋ The North or South? game (previous page) is a good warm-up to Battle of the Brains because it familiarizes students with the information on the cards. Many of the facts in North or South? are echoed in the Battle of the Brains questions.

❋ Photocopy the side 1A and 1B cards (pages 67 and 68) back to back onto card stock or stiff paper. Photocopy the side 2A and 2B cards (pages 69 and 70) back to back on the same type of paper. *Note that correctly aligning double-sided copies may be difficult.* One alternative is to make permanent cards from the pages of this book (be sure to keep additional copies of these pages on hand!): simply laminate the aligned back-to-back pages (67/68 and 69/70), cut out the cards, and store them for future use in an envelope. Another option is to photocopy each page, correctly align the paired pages back to back, and glue them together.

❋ Cut out all the cards on the solid lines and fold them in half on the dotted lines to form tents. The FACT sides should be facing out; the questions should be on the inside.

❋ Assign each team a side—either North or South. Put the NORTH card directly in front of the North team and the SOUTH card in front of the South team. The BOTH card goes in the center

of the playing space.

⭐ Classify the rest of the cards into three groups: North, South, Both. (See label on the inside of the cards.) Place the BOTH cards in the center of the playing space, sideways, so that each team can see the point values (Infantry or Cavalry). Each team places its cards so that the FACT sides are facing the opponent and the point sides are hidden from the opponent's view.

How to Play the Game

⭐ To take a turn, a player taps (but does not pick up) either an opponent's card or a card in the BOTH area.

⭐ The opponent picks up the card and reads the inside. There are several types of cards:

★ *Questions:* If the player answers a question correctly, he or she wins the card. If not, the card stays in play. The opponent places it back in place, according to the type of card.

★ *Bombs* (North and South categories only): The player scores no points. Bombs stay in play, so players should make a mental note of where they are. Players can only move their cards to read questions or replace them after an incorrect question.

★ *Spy* (Both category only): The player keeps the card and scores bonus points at the end of the game.

★ *Presidents* (North and South categories only): As soon as a player picks a "president" card, the game is over.

⭐ Players tally the points on the cards they have won, adding bonus points for choosing a president or a spy. The higher scorer wins.

Variations

Strategic Play: Here are some strategy tips to share with students:

★ Pay attention to the facts in the North or South? game. Information on these fact cards often reappears as a question in Battle of the Brains.

★ Choosing BOTH cards is a safer bet than choosing an opponent's cards. BOTH cards don't contain any bombs, and the point values are not hidden, meaning students can choose a harder or easier card depending on their skill level. Also, students can earn bonus points if they happen to pick the spy.

★ An opponent's cards are riskier, but can yield more points per turn. They include a 5-point officer card and a 5-point bonus for choosing the president.

Longer Game: Play until both presidents have been chosen.

North or South Fact Cards ★

Note: Infantry, Cavalry, and Officer points are used only in the Battle of the Brains game.

Side 1A

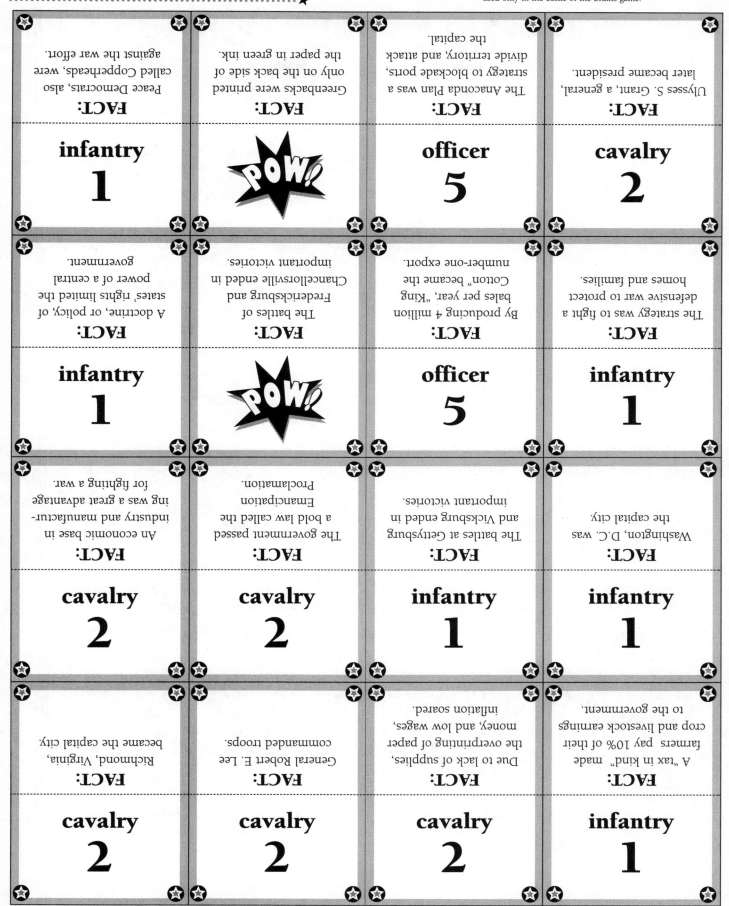

FACT: Peace Democrats, also called Copperheads, were against the war effort.

infantry 1

FACT: Greenbacks were printed only on the back side of the paper in green ink.

POW!

FACT: The Anaconda Plan was a strategy to blockade ports, divide territory, and attack the capital.

officer 5

FACT: Ulysses S. Grant, a general, later became president.

cavalry 2

FACT: A doctrine, or policy, of states' rights limited the power of a central government.

infantry 1

FACT: The battles of Fredericksburg and Chancellorsville ended in important victories.

POW!

FACT: By producing 4 million bales per year, "King Cotton" became the number-one export.

officer 5

FACT: The strategy was to fight a defensive war to protect homes and families.

infantry 1

FACT: An economic base in industry and manufacturing was a great advantage for fighting a war.

cavalry 2

FACT: The government passed a bold law called the Emancipation Proclamation.

cavalry 2

FACT: The battles at Gettysburg and Vicksburg ended in important victories.

infantry 1

FACT: Washington, D.C. was the capital city.

infantry 1

FACT: Richmond, Virginia, became the capital city.

cavalry 2

FACT: General Robert E. Lee commanded troops.

cavalry 2

FACT: Due to lack of supplies, the overprinting of paper money, and low wages, inflation soared.

cavalry 2

FACT: A "tax in kind" made farmers pay 10% of their crop and livestock earnings to the government.

infantry 1

NORTH

Q: Name three of the five border states.

A: Delaware, Kentucky, Missouri, Maryland, and West Virginia (became a state in 1863).

NORTH

Q: What government cabinet did Salmon P. Chase head?

A: Treasury. His Legal Tender Act allowed the Union to print $150 million in greenbacks to pay for the war.

NORTH

You lose this turn.

Place this Bomb Card back on the North game board.

NORTH

Q: What was a border state?

A: A slave state that stayed with the Union.

SOUTH

Q: The 1862 battle between the *Monitor* and the *Virginia* was the first meeting of what type of new ship?

A: Ironclads. For four hours, cannonballs bounced harmlessly off both iron hulls.

SOUTH

Q: Name the riot started by hungry women in Richmond, Virginia.

A: The Bread Riot. Women cried, "Bread! Bread!" and smashed windows to protest high food costs. Jefferson Davis stopped the riot.

SOUTH

You lose this turn.

Place this Bomb Card back on the South game board.

SOUTH

Q: What were blockade runners?

A: Ships that smuggled supplies through the Union blockade of southern harbors.

NORTH

Q: What was the main reason that people in northern cities rioted?

A: The draft. In the four-day New York City Draft Riot, people burned and looted local African-American buildings and terrorized the African-American population.

NORTH

Q: What was a green-back?

A: Paper money first issued by the U.S. government in 1861. The backside was usually printed in green ink.

NORTH

Q: Name three of six exemptions (excuses) not to serve in the Confederate Army.

A: Age (17–50 years), gender (men only), job skills needed at home, disability, money (pay-offs), owning 20+ slaves.

NORTH

Q: Why were bounties less successful in the North than in the South?

A: Some volunteers took the bounty money and deserted at the first chance.

SOUTH

Q: Though the South won at Chancellorsville, it lost what top leader?

A: Gen. Thomas "Stonewall" Jackson. His own troops shot him by accident in the arm. He later died of pneumonia.

SOUTH

Q: A union of states in which the central government has limited power is called what?

A: A confederacy. For example, eight Confederate states passed individual income tax laws.

SOUTH

Q: What was the first state to secede from the Union on December 20, 1860?

A: South Carolina. Mississippi, Florida, Alabama, Georgia, Louisiana, and Texas followed shortly afterward.

SOUTH

Q: After the bombing of Fort Sumter, name two of the four southern states that seceded from the Union.

A: Virginia (except for 46 counties), North Carolina, Tennessee, Arkansas.

North or South Fact Cards ★

Note: Infantry, Cavalry, and Officer points are used only in the Battle of the Brains game.

Side 2A

Card 1 (Row 1, Col 1)
FACT: The slave states of Delaware, Maryland, Kentucky, Missouri, and West Virginia were border states.
infantry 1

Card 2 (Row 1, Col 2)
U.S. President Abraham Lincoln
FACT: The blockade was a string of warships that captured or deterred supply ships going to and from ports.

Card 3 (Row 1, Col 3)
FACT: Ironclads, ships with a thick cover of iron, were deadly to wooden warships of the day.
infantry 1

Card 4 (Row 1, Col 4)
FACT: In 1863, citizens in cities rioted.
infantry 1

Card 5 (Row 2, Col 1)
FACT: States seceded from the U.S.A. to form the Confederate States of America.
infantry 1

Card 6 (Row 2, Col 2)
Confederate President Jefferson Davis
FACT: Blockade runners snuck in supplies.

Card 7 (Row 2, Col 3)
FACT: The military offered men a bounty, or payment, for joining the army as volunteers.
cavalry 2

Card 8 (Row 2, Col 4)
FACT: A conscription, or draft, required men to serve in the military.
infantry 1

Card 9 (Row 3, Col 1)
FACT: For each soldier killed in battle, two soldiers died of diseases such as dysentery, scurvy, and typhoid.
cavalry 2

Card 10 (Row 3, Col 2)
FACT: Due to heavy casualties, trains were converted into traveling hospitals.
infantry 1

Card 11 (Row 3, Col 3)
FACT: Artillery such as the Howitzer required many horses to transport and well-trained soldiers to use.
infantry 1

Card 12 (Row 3, Col 4)
FACT: Women served as spies.
infantry 1

Card 13 (Row 4, Col 1)
FACT: At camps such as Elmira and Andersonville, many prisoners of war died of starvation and disease.
infantry 1

Card 14 (Row 4, Col 2)
NORTH (TEAM 2)
NORTH (TEAM 1)

Card 15 (Row 4, Col 3)
SOUTH (TEAM 2)
SOUTH (TEAM 1)

Card 16 (Row 4, Col 4)
BOTH (TEAM 2)
BOTH (TEAM 1)

BOTH

Q: Robert E. Lee surrendered at Appomattox to what Union general?

A: Ulysses S. Grant. Grant's rank of three-star lieutenant general had been awarded only once, to George Washington.

BOTH

Q: "Sherman's March to the Sea" ended in what coastal city of Georgia?

A: Savannah. Union soldiers destroyed southern crops, railroads, bridges, homes, and entire cities.

NORTH

The Civil War Is Over!

Award 5 bonus points to the South. Then total your scores to see who won.

NORTH

Q: A venomous snake and the head of Liberty on a penny gave rise to what nickname for a political group?

A: The Copperheads. These Peace Democrats wore the penny as a badge.

BOTH

Spy!

Your spy, disguised as an infantryman, gathered intelligence behind enemy lines.

Earn 3 points instead of 1.

BOTH

Q: Farm soldiers caught more childhood diseases such as mumps and measles than city soldiers. Why?

A: On farms, they were not exposed to many diseases, and so did not build up immunities.

SOUTH

The Civil War Is Over!

Award 5 bonus points to the North. Then total your scores to see who won.

SOUTH

Q: Who was Belle Boyd?

A: A southern spy. At age 18, she smuggled messages for Stonewall Jackson. She was caught on a blockade runner, but married a Union officer to escape.

BOTH

Q: At first, Britain supported the South because it needed what raw material?

A: Cotton. After the Emancipation Proclamation to free slaves, Britain withdrew its support.

BOTH

Q: What law freed only those slaves in rebelling states, but not slaves in border states?

A: The Emancipation Proclamation. Abraham Lincoln did not want to risk losing the support of the border states.

BOTH

Q: In Pennsylvania, rebels in search of shoes ran into Yankees, starting what big battle?

A: Gettysburg. In a key turning point, southern troops retreated after Pickett's charge failed.

BOTH

Q: A victory at what city gave the Union control of the Mississippi River?

A: Vicksburg. After a long siege, the Rebels surrendered on July 4, 1863. Vicksburg didn't celebrate Independence Day for 81 years.

BOTH / BOTH

SOUTH / SOUTH

NORTH / NORTH

BOTH

Q: Robert E. Lee turned down command of Union troops to defend his home state. What was the state?

A: Virginia. Lee drove back Union troops, who came within 7 miles of Richmond, Virginia.

Civil War Research Game

Spy Versus Spy

☙ A Top Secret Internet and Book Search Challenge ❧

Teams of players are espionage agents who use their research skills to compile dossiers on enemy spies of the Civil War. The more complete their dossiers, the higher their score.

Materials

🛡 Spy Versus Spy dossier form (page 51)

Players: 2 or more individuals or teams (3 to 6 students per team)

Objectives

Historical Perspective (Comprehending the Past; Analyzing and Interpreting the Past) and Inquiry (Conducting Investigations): Work cooperatively to research biographical information about figures in history.

Language Arts: Write a dossier, including primary source quotations.

Preparation

✹ Make several copies per player or team of the dossier form.

✹ Gather references about people in the Civil War. (See "Book Links.")

✹ Bookmark Web sites with information about people in the Civil War. (See "Web Links.")

✹ Copy and review the sample dossier on Jacques Cousteau (page 52).

How to Play the Game

Rules for playing are the same as those on pages 48 and 49, under "Spy Versus Spy: Revolutionary War." Here's a reference list of Civil War spies. The starred spies are easier to research, since more has been written about them.

UNION/YANKEE

Lafayette Curry Baker

Pauline Cushman (stage name of Harriet Wood)

*Sarah Emma Edmonds

*Allen Pinkerton (founder of the Pinkerton
   Detective Agency)

*Elizabeth Van Lew

Mary Elizabeth Bowser

Grenville Mellon Dodge

Thomas McNiven

John Scobell (Pinkerton agent)

George H. Sharpe (Grant's spy chief)

Timothy Webster (Pinkerton agent)

CONFEDERATE/REBEL

George A. Atzerodt (accomplice of
John Wilkes Booth)

*Rose O'Neal Greenhow ("the Rose
   of Washington")

*"Belle" Boyd ("La Belle Rebelle")

Sam Davis ("the Confederate Nathan Hale")

Nancy Hart

Richard Thomas Robert Cobb Kennedy

CIA Kids Page: www.odci.gov/cia/ciakids/history and
CIA Documents: www.odci.gov/cia/publications/dispatches/dispatch
Biographical information about a few famous spies in history. For more
information, write to Public Affairs, CIA, Washington, DC 20505.

Duke University (primary documents): scriptorium.lib.duke.edu
Click on "Civil War Women," which is listed under the heading "Digitized
collections." Alternately, you can search the Duke University site for "Civil
War Women" or specific names of spies.

Institute for Advanced Technology in the Humanities:
jefferson.village.virginia.edu
A site search for the name of a spy or the word "spy" yields a long list of
19th-century newspaper articles under the page heading "Valley of the
Shadow" and a few other archival pages. For example, Pauline Cushman's
thrilling adventures were printed in the June 1964 edition of the newspaper.

Yahoo for Kids: www.yahooligans.com
Click on "School Bell," "Social Studies," "History," and "United States
History" (in that order). Then search for "spies" or for specific names of
spies (note: change the pull-down menu from "all of Yahooligans" to "just
this category"). Kids can do a similar search using other browsers such as
about.com, kidsinfo.com, and ajkids.com.

BOOK LINKS

Civil War Cards
(Atlas Editions, 1995)
We use this set every
year throughout the
Civil War unit.

CHAPTER 4

The Progressive Era

Muckraker

🦅 A Progressive Era Board Game 🦅

Players zip around a game board, answering questions in four categories (Everyday Life, Labor and Business, Famous People, Government). They also give to charity, greedily take from the "rich," and perform brief vaudeville acts!

Players: 2 to 4 players

Materials

🛡 Muckraker game board (pages 79 and 80)
🛡 Muckraker cards (pages 75–78)
🛡 playing pieces (one per player), 1 die

Objective

Civic Perspective: Identify problems and solutions that affect the public good. Interpret core democratic values of justice, equality, public or common good, and truth.

Preparation

✴ Copy and laminate the game board (pages 79 and 80) and attach it to the inside of a file folder. Use markers to color the Labor & Business space blue, the Government space green, and the Famous People space pink. Leave the Everyday Life space white.

✴ Copy each page of cards onto different-colored paper (white, blue, green, or pink) as indicated at the top of the page.

✴ Place the cards, playing pieces, and die in an envelope and put the envelope in the file folder for easy storage.

✴ When students are ready to play, shuffle all the cards together and place them in three roughly equal stacks on the game board.

How to Play the Game

✴ All players start on the middle space and take turns clockwise.

✴ To take a turn, a player rolls the die and moves his or her playing piece in any direction.

(Playing pieces can't move back and forth between two spaces; they must continue in a forward direction.) Here's what landing on each type of space means:

- ★ *Blank Space:* Do nothing; the turn is over.
- ★ *Pure Greed:* Take one card from the opponent who owns the most cards. If there's a tie, the player gets to choose which opponent must give up a card. (Of course, if no one has cards, the player doesn't get to take any.)
- ★ *Charity:* Give one card to the opponent who owns the least number of cards. Again, if there's a tie, the player can choose the opponent, and if the player has no cards, he or she doesn't have to give anything away.
- ★ *Roll Again:* Roll the die again and take another turn.
- ★ *Vaudeville:* Put on a little act and get warm applause as a reward. (Vaudeville was a major form of entertainment during the Progressive Era.)
- ★ *Category Space:* Answer a question by following rule 3. Players don't need an exact roll to land on a category space. They simply stop and give up any remaining moves on the die.

BOOK LINKS

Kids at Work: Lewis Hine and the Crusade Against Child Labor by Russell Freedman (Clarion, 1998). Famous photographs of child workers taken by a muckraker. Like Freedman's other history books, this one will fascinate children.

3 Players who land on a category space can answer a question in that category only if a matching card is on top of one of the three decks. Example: Suppose a player lands on "Famous People" (pink) and a pink card is on top of one deck. The opponent to the left of the player draws the card and asks the question. If the player answers correctly, he or she keeps the card. If the player gets it wrong, the card goes on the bottom the deck. In either case, the turn ends. If two pink cards are on the tops of two decks, the player can try to win both of them. If three are showing (one on top of each deck), the player can go for a hat trick—three cards on one turn. If no pink cards are showing, the player does nothing on that turn. On the player's next turn, he or she must roll and leave the category space.

4 The first player to own ten cards is the winner. Alternately, the player with the greatest number of cards at the end of a time limit is the winner.

Variations

Discuss Strategy: The categories of the top cards change throughout the game. Players must zip from one corner to another to reach category spaces before someone else snaps up the matching cards. There's no point in landing on a category space that does not have a matching card showing. Players can either hover around such a space until a matching card pops up, or they can head for another category.

Landing on Other Players: If a player lands on an opponent's spot with an exact roll of the die, he or she can win one of the opponent's cards. The opponent chooses any card that he or she owns and reads the question aloud. If the player answers correctly, he or she takes the card. If the answer is wrong, nothing happens, and the turn ends.

Muckraker Everyday Life Cards

Everyday Life

After working in slums, Dr. S. Josephine Baker said, "It's six times safer to be a soldier in the trenches of France than to be ____."

a. a corrupt politician
b. an immigrant
c. *a baby in the U.S.*
d. a poor person

Everyday Life

During the Progressive Era (1870s to 1920), where did populations increase the fastest?

a. *in cities**
b. on farms
c. in suburbs
d. none of the above

*centers of progressivism

Everyday Life

Which sport was *not* invented in the late 1800s?

a. pro football   (1895)
b. basketball   (1890)
c. pro baseball   (1869)
d. *soccer*   *(centuries old)*

Everyday Life

In the 1870s, what German innovation spread to the U.S. and still exists today?

a. assembly line
b. *kindergarten*
c. welfare
d. meat inspection

Everyday Life

People began to pay a graduated income tax in the Progressive Era. How was it graduated?

a. *the rich paid a higher percentage of their income*
b. only the rich paid
c. it wasn't due all at once
d. only college grads paid

Everyday Life

What killed more than 140 people at the Triangle Shirtwaist Company factory in 1911?

a. contaminated meat
b. *too few exits during a fire*
c. mob riot after a strike
d. a tornado

Everyday Life

Compulsory attendance laws required what group to show up at certain times?

a. workers at factories
b. *children at school*
c. senators in Congress
d. voters at elections

Everyday Life

How did labor-saving inventions affect life in the Progressive Era?

a. *Leisure time increased.*
b. The workday became longer.
c. Workers lost jobs to robots.
d. There was no effect at all.

Everyday Life

Why didn't most rural people go to doctors' offices for treatment?

a. *Doctors came to them.*
b. All doctors lived in cities.
c. Farmers were too poor.
d. All of the above.

Everyday Life

What was vaudeville (VAWD-vihl)?

a. an entertainment city
b. a silent movie studio
c. *staged variety shows with songs, comedy, magic, juggling, etc.*
d. variety shows on radio

Everyday Life

What did settlement houses such as Hull House offer?

a. settlement of disputes
b. *social services to the poor and immigrants*
c. bomb-proof shelters
d. a meeting place for corrupt politicians

Everyday Life

What kind of wage did a teenage girl make in a sweatshop at the turn of the century?

a. *a few dollars per week*
b. a few dollars per day
c. a few dollars per hour
d. minimum wage set by law

Everyday Life

In 1900, city hospitals were mainly used for what group of people?

a. the rich*
b. *the poor*
c. the incurable
d. mothers giving birth

*They could afford private doctors.

Everyday Life

Starting in 1900, state laws banned child labor, thanks to Florence Kelley. When did a federal child labor law take effect?

a. 1910s
b. *1920s*
c. *1930s*
d. never

Everyday Life

The term *muckraker* comes from *muckrake*. What is a muckrake?

a. *rake for raking muck, mud, or dung*
b. rakish (stylish) man
c. tool for writing
d. fine-toothed comb

Everyday Life

In what famous book did muckraker Upton Sinclair observe that sausages had poisoned rats, sawdust, dirt, and germs in them?

a. "Animal Farm"
b. "The Meatpackers"
c. *The Jungle* (Read it!)
d. "Shame in the Cities"

Labor & Business

What was *not* a big business in the late 19th century?

a. steel
b. railroads and shipping
c. *automobiles*
d. coal mining

Labor & Business

The Grangers were a cooperative organization of what type of rural worker?

a. *farmers*
b. children
c. government forest rangers
d. meat grinders

Labor & Business

How did the Sherman Antitrust Act affect trade (buying and selling)?

a. opened foreign markets
b. restrained (limited) trade
c. *opened trade by banning monopolies*
d. set up monopolies

Labor & Business

The Interstate Commerce Act of 1887 set up the first regulatory commission to control what corrupt industry?

a. *railroads*
b. airlines
c. peddlers (vendors)
d. textiles

Labor & Business

What word does *not* describe labor leader Samuel Gompers?

a. immigrant
b. pro-union*
c. *anti-union*
d. cigar maker

*He founded the American Federation of Labor (AFL)

Labor & Business

What is *not* a trust?

a. a monopoly
b. a big business run by a board of trustees who control company stock
c. a group of businesses that control a product or service
d. *a mom-and-pop shop*

Labor & Business

In sweatshops, workers did piecework for long hours. What's piecework?

a. making very tiny parts
b. any underpaid labor
c. *payment per finished item, such as a shirt*
d. bonus for illegal work

Labor & Business

The Sherman Antitrust Act banned monopolies. What is a monopoly?

a. private bank
b. *complete control over a market, product, or service*
c. price fixing (agreement to set high prices)
d. real estate fraud

Labor & Business

How did "laissez-faire" policies apply to businesses?

a. *let them run with little government restriction*
b. imposed strict laws
c. banned imports
d. set price controls

Labor & Business

What abuse by big businesses did muckrakers *not* expose?

a. monopolies that kept prices high
b. *nonpayment of federal income taxes*
c. harmful products
d. dangerous workplaces

Labor & Business

What did most sweatshops make (besides money)?

a. machines
b. *clothing*
c. automobiles
d. food

Labor & Business

How do workers' compensation laws help workers?

a. set a minimum wage
b. let workers sue bosses
c. ensure paid vacation
d. *compensate workers injured on the job*

Labor & Business

What did the Knights of Labor oppose?

a. an 8-hour work day
b. *striking*
c. safety rules
d. one union for many trades ("all who toiled")

Labor & Business

What's a definition of a labor strike?

a. poor working conditions
b. violent protest
c. *planned work stoppage by workers*
d. overtime

Labor & Business

What's a boycott?

a. labor strike
b. Progressive Era boy scout
c. child worker
d. *campaign not to buy a product or service to protest a company*

Labor & Business

How did inventions that helped farmers produce more crops also hurt farmers?

a. machines were costly
b. the price of crops dropped from oversupply
c. only big farms with one crop made money
d. *all of the above*

Famous People

Which title does *not* apply to Emma Goldman?

a. "the most dangerous woman in America"*
b. immigrant
c. *communist*
d. anarchist (opponent of all forms of government)

*for inciting violence

Famous People

What did Ida B. Wells write that caused her newspaper to be bombed?

a. threats against political bosses
b. *articles against lynching (illegal hanging)*
c. pro-communism letters
d. anti-war editorials

Famous People

Who was *not* a muckraker (a writer who investigates and exposes wrongdoing)?

a. Upton Sinclair
b. Nellie Bly
c. *J.P. Morgan   (banker)*
d. Ida Tarbell

Famous People

Who did *not* live in the Progressive Era (roughly 1870s to 1920) ?

a. *Lucille Ball, TV star*
b. Scott Joplin, ragtime musician
c. Beatrix Potter, author
d. John Philip Sousa, composer of marches

Famous People

What did Booker T. Washington say was the key to fighting racism?

a. violence
b. peaceful protest
c. *self-improvement, especially through education*
d. integration

* He founded the Tuskegee Institute for higher education.

Famous People

What "evil" did Carry Nation try to stamp out with her ax?

a. rats and other vermin in city streets
b. *drinking alcohol*
c. poorly built tenements
d. sweatshops

*She hacked up bars.

Famous People

Samuel Hopkins Adams wrote that many medicines were harmful drugs. What act did he inspire?

a. Food Inspection Act
b. Drug Rehab Act
c. *Pure Food & Drug Act*
d. Truth in Advertising Act

Famous People

Which president was *not* in office during the Progressive Era?

a. Theodore Roosevelt
b. Woodrow Wilson
c. *Franklin Delano Roosevelt (1933–1945)*
d. William Howard Taft

Famous People

The motto of Governor Robert "Battling Bob" La Follette was "The will of the people shall be _____."

a. *the law of the land*
b. no concern of mine
c. second only to the will of government
d. heard in Washington

Famous People

W.E.B. Du Bois said, "The way for people to gain their reasonable rights is _____."

a. to politely ask for them.
b. *not to voluntarily throw them away.*
c. to elect me president.
d. to segregate.

Famous People

Which fact is *not* true about Jane Addams?

a. *She argued for U.S. entry into World War I.*
b. She co-founded Hull House.
c. She won the Nobel Peace Prize.
d. She co-founded the American Civil Liberties Union.

Famous People

What profession did Louisa May Alcott and L. Frank Baum share?

a. muckraker
b. *author (of children's books)*
c. politician
d. reformer

Famous People

People joked that William Taft's name stood for **T**ake **A**dvice **F**rom whom?

a. Boss Tweed, a corrupt politician
b. *Teddy (Roosevelt), also a progressive*
c. Traitors
d. Tippy, his dog

Famous People

About Carrie Chapman Catt, a reporter wrote, "To see her is like looking at sheer marble, flame-lit." Who was she?

a. a striking statue
b. a fiery anarchist
c. *a fiery suffragist*
d. a fiery First Lady

Famous People

George Bellows was one of many "Ashcan School" artists. What did his paintings portray?

a. antismoking messages
b. antiwar messages
c. factory conditions
d. *slum life*

Famous People

Who was William "Boss" Tweed of New York City?

a. a textile factory owner who abused workers
b. *a powerful and corrupt New York politician*
c. a political cartoonist
d. a labor leader

Muckraker Government Cards

Government

What business does the Federal Reserve System* regulate?

a. unions
b. textiles
c. *banking*
d. transportation

*created under Woodrow Wilson

Government

In 1913, Congress added the 16th amendment to the Constitution to pay for reforms. What was it about?

a. outlawing slavery
b. women's right to vote
c. civil rights for all
d. *a federal income tax*

Government

What was the goal of Wilson's 1913 "New Freedom" program?

a. to free all slaves
b. *to stop unfair practices by big businesses*
c. to free big businesses to run as they saw fit
d. to feed the poor

Government

Before the 17th amendment (1913), how were senators selected?

a. *chosen by state legislatures*
b. elected by judges
c. elected by the people
d. chosen by the president

Government

What did so-called "machine politicians" like Boss Tweed often do?

a. gun down enemies
b. *stuff ballot boxes to ensure election*
c. fight for labor laws in machine shops
d. shut down sweatshops

Government

The Pure Food and Drug Act banned harmful additives to food and medicine. What else did it ban?

a. *false advertising*
b. foreign foods
c. price gouging or fixing
d. fake expiration dates

Government

To give voters power, progressives introduced initiatives. What are they?

a. voter education drives
b. *the right to introduce legislation*
c. vetoes of bills
d. recalls of elected officials

Government

A referendum gives voters more power than an initiative. What is it?

a. *right of citizens to vote directly on proposed laws*
b. a recall of a governor
c. veto power to stop bills
d. refusal to pay taxes

Government

What is the "shame" in *The Shame of the Cities,* by Lincoln Steffens?

a. rat-infested tenements
b. long hours for child workers
c. *government corruption (bribery, for example)*
d. crime

Government

Which group could not legally vote in a national election until 1920?

a. *women*
b. African Americans*
c. 18-year-olds**
d. communists

*Right granted in 1870
** Right granted in 1971

Government

Which group did *not* oppose women voting?

a. political bosses
b. *suffragists**
c. Catholic church
d. liquor industry

*They fought *for* it, forming the National Women's Party.

Government

In 1896, what did the Supreme Court rule in *Plessy v. Ferguson*?

a. "Jim Crow" was guilty.
b. Slavery was illegal.
c. Lynching was illegal.
d. *Facilities for blacks and whites were to be "separate but equal."*

Government

Many political bosses took bribes in exchange for favors, such as job contracts. What's a bribe?

a. a salary bonus
b. *illegal payoff*
c. a guaranteed vote in the next election
d. legal payoff

Government

When the coal miners' union went on strike in 1902, Teddy Roosevelt took the side of _____.

a. foreign business
b. the mine owners
c. *the union workers*
d. the nonunion workers

Government

Teddy Roosevelt won the 1904 election by promising what kind of "Square Deal"?

a. welfare for the poor
b. lower income tax
c. women's right to vote
d. *an equal chance for everyone to succeed*

Government

As a conservationist, Teddy Roosevelt said, "The rights of the public to natural resources outweigh" what rights?

a. animal rights
b. *private rights*
c. women's rights
d. all rights everywhere

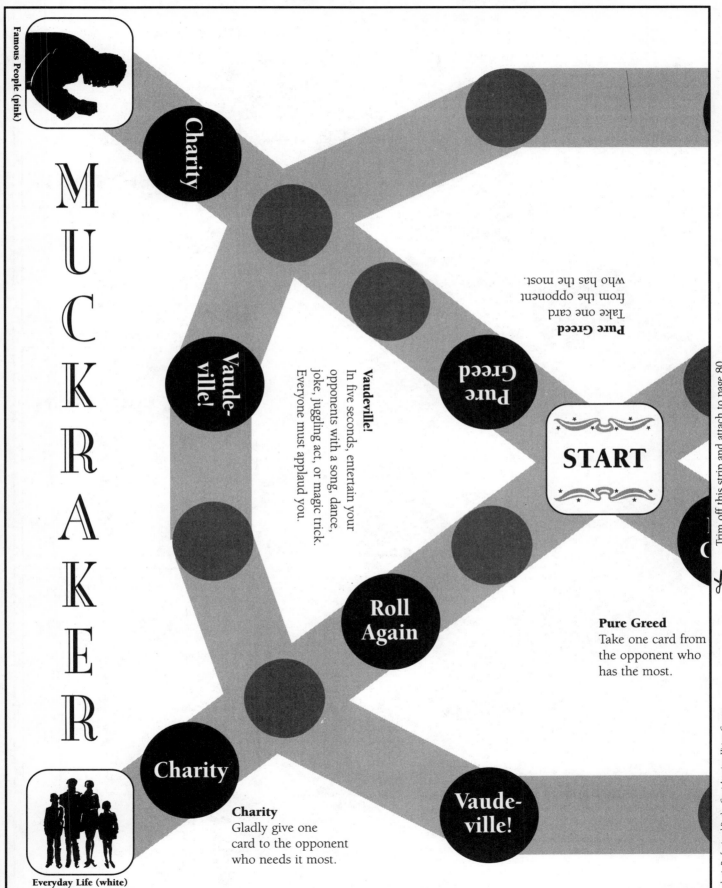

Famous People (pink)

MUCKRAKER

Charity

Vaude-ville!

Vaudeville!
In five seconds, entertain your opponents with a song, dance, joke, juggling act, or magic trick. Everyone must applaud you.

Pure Greed

Pure Greed
Take one card from the opponent who has the most.

START

Roll Again

Charity
Gladly give one card to the opponent who needs it most.

Charity

Vaude-ville!

Everyday Life (white)

Trim off this strip and attach to page 80.

Pure Greed
Take one card from the opponent who has the most.

Scholastic Professional books, *Great American History Games*

Labor & Business (blue)

Vaude-ville!

Charity
Gladly give one card to the opponent who needs it most.

Charity

Roll Again

Vaudeville!
In five seconds, entertain your opponents with a song, dance, joke, juggling act, or magic trick. Everyone must applaud you.

Pure Greed

Vaude-ville!

MUCKRAKER

Charity

Government (green)

MUCKRAKER

Question Cards

?

MUCKRAKER

Question Cards

?

MUCKRAKER

Question Cards

?